WOODEN MONUMENTAL EFFIGIES
IN ENGLAND AND WALES

PRIEST IN EUCHARISTIC VESTMENTS (*c.* 1280).
CLIFFORD, HEREFORDSHIRE.

WOODEN
MONUMENTAL EFFIGIES
IN
ENGLAND AND WALES

BY

ALFRED C. FRYER, Ph.D., F.S.A.

MEMBER OF COUNCIL OF THE ROYAL ARCHÆOLOGICAL INSTITUTE
VICE-PRESIDENT OF THE BRISTOL AND GLOUCESTERSHIRE ARCHÆOLOGICAL SOCIETY
MEMBER OF THE SOMERSET ARCHÆOLOGICAL SOCIETY

NEW, REVISED AND ENLARGED EDITION

SIXTY-SEVEN ILLUSTRATIONS FROM ORIGINAL PHOTOGRAPHS

LONDON: ELLIOT STOCK
7 PATERNOSTER ROW E.C
MCMXXIV

PREFACE

ON the 26th November, 1908, I had the honour of reading a paper on *The Wooden Monumental Effigies in England and Wales* before The Society of Antiquaries, and it was published in volume LXI of *Archæologia* (pp. 487–552). The Society of Antiquaries kindly granted permission for the republishing of this paper as a single volume, and to make it more instructive it was freely illustrated by a series of photographs taken by myself, with the exception of the Chew Magna effigy, which was the work of Mr. F. Bromhead, of Clifton, and the Fersfield effigy, which was specially photographed by the Rev. G. F. Sharland, Vicar of Binham, Norfolk, who had the pews removed for that purpose.

This edition was published fifteen years ago, and The Society of Antiquaries has again granted my request to permit Mr. Elliot Stock, of Paternoster Row, London, to bring out a second edition. This new edition contains all the illustrations used in the earlier volume, with the addition of 21 blocks made from my own photographs. To supplement my own collection of illustrations I have had the assistance of Mr. Arthur Gardner, M.A., F.S.A., who has generously allowed blocks to be made for this volume for Figures 5, 6, 10, 15, 25, 31, 32, 41, 42, 47, and 48 from his own beautiful photographs.

Two more wooden effigies have been discovered since 1908, and notes on these are inserted in this volume, while the text and the topographical index have been expanded so as to embrace the views of those who have written on this particular subject since my paper was first read before The Society of Antiquaries.

References are made to two effigies which must be added to those that we know have been destroyed, so that there are twenty-four which have disappeared and ninety-six still existing in twenty-seven English and Welsh counties.

CLIFTON,
 BRISTOL.

CONTENTS

PART I

PART II

CONTENTS

PART III

LIST OF ILLUSTRATIONS

PLATE I.

Fig. 1.

ROBERT, DUKE OF NORMANDY. EFFIGY (*c.* 1280). GLOUCESTER CATHEDRAL.

Fig. 2.

WILLIAM OF VALENCE (DIED 1296). WESTMINSTER ABBEY.

PART I

INTRODUCTORY

THE forty-sixth volume of *Archæologia* contains a paper on Little Horkesley Church, Essex, by Sir Clement R. Markham, with some account of the three wooden monumental effigies in that church.[1] A carefully prepared list of the wooden monumental effigies in England and Wales is appended to that paper. This list is arranged as a topographical index, and records the existence of seventy-eight wooden effigies. Four, however, are given in error, so that this number is reduced to seventy-four. Recent research now permits twenty-two more to be added to this list. Sir Clement R. Markham only refers to six wooden effigies which were destroyed; records of nineteen more, however, are now appended, and it is quite probable that this unfortunate list may have to be extended as further knowledge of our lost effigies comes to light.

Some notices of wooden monumental effigies are found in the work of the industrious Weever, who studied effigies in the dioceses of Canterbury, London, and Rochester in the seventeenth century. Gough's stately folios on *Sepulchral Monuments in Great Britain*; Stothard's great work on *Monumental Effigies*, which was brought to a conclusion by his untimely death in 1821; the Rev. Thomas Kerrich's beautiful drawings now preserved in the British Museum; Mr. Albert Hartshorne's splendid work on the *Recumbent Monumental Effigies of Northamptonshire*; Mr.

[1] Pp. 269–80.

Chancellor's *Ancient Sepulchral Monuments of Essex*; the volumes of Lyson's *Magna Britannia*; and the beautiful work of the brothers Hollis, have all given us some illustrations and scattered references to a few of our wooden effigies.

The county histories contain a few records of this class of monumental effigies; for example, the paper on the effigy of Robert du Bois, at Fersfield, Norfolk, by Blomefield,[1] is of value, and there is a long account of the effigy of Sir John Pitchford in Eyton's *Shropshire*.[2] The most valuable paper on wooden effigies in the county histories is to be found in the first volume of the new *Victoria History of Northamptonshire*,[3] by the late Mr. Albert Hartshorne, whose wide and extensive knowledge was so freely at the service of the author of this paper. Since this volume was written Professor Prior and Mr. Arthur Gardner's splendid work on *Medieval Figure Sculpture in England* has been published, and the section devoted to "The Oak Effigies"[4] is more than once referred to in this new edition of the paper the author read before The Society of Antiquaries in 1908. *Notes and Queries* contains a few useful references, and the transactions of the county archæological societies contain papers on a few individual wooden effigies. Mr. Henry Laver has written on the Elmstead knight,[5] Canon Bazeley and Miss M. L. Bazeley on the effigy of Robert, Duke of Normandy, in Gloucester cathedral church,[6] the late Sir William Hope on a wooden effigy and tomb of a secular canon in the church of All Saints, Derby,[7] while in the volumes of the *Archæological Journal* a paper is found on the effigy of a priest at Little Leighs, Essex,[8] on four wooden effigies at Clifton Reynes, Buck-

[1] Vol. I, 104.   [2] Vol. II, 282.
[3] Vol. I, 400.   [4] Pp. 661–71.
[5] *Transactions of the Essex Archæological Society*, X, Part 3.
[6] *Transactions of the Bristol and Gloucestershire Archæological Society*, XXVII, 289.
[7] *Transactions of the Derbyshire Archæological and Natural History Society*, VIII, 185.   [8] Vol. XVIII, 77.

PLATE II.

PLATE II.

Fig. 3.

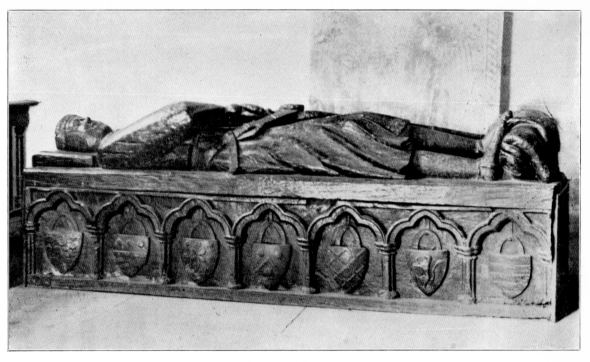

SIR JOHN PITCHFORD (DIED 1285).   PITCHFORD, SHROPSHIRE.

Fig. 4.

MARGARET, 2ND WIFE OF ADAM OF EVERINGHAM (*c.* 1290).   LAXTON, NOTTINGHAMSHIRE.

inghamshire,[1] and the cross-legged effigy of a layman at Much Marcle, Herefordshire,[2] has been carefully described by Mr. Bloxam. The *Transactions of the Exeter Diocesan Architectural Society* [3] contain a paper on the wooden effigy of a lady at Tawstock, Devon ; the *Transactions of the Woolhope Naturalists' Field Club* possess a valuable paper on the " Wooden Monumental Effigies of Herefordshire," by Mr. George Marshall, F.S.A. ; but by far the most important work on effigies in wood is the paper by Mr. Albert Hartshorne in *Some Minor Arts,*[4] published in 1894.

As far as can be at present ascertained there are ninety-six wooden monumental effigies existing [5] in England and Wales, and these are distributed over twenty-seven counties.[6] Fifty-nine are military personages, and among them we find one duke and three earls. There are twenty-four ladies, and of their number four are countesses. We have also one king, one judge, three laymen, one archbishop and four priests, and three of the effigies have cadavers, in addition to a cadaver which now possesses no effigy.

Authentic records exist of twenty-four wooden effigies which have been destroyed, and these were located in thirteen different counties.[7] Thirteen were military personages, including one

---

[1] Vol. XI, 149. [2] Vol. XXXIII, 239.
[3] Vol. VI, 192. [4] Pp. 55–67.

[5] The wooden figures of William of Valence and King Henry V in Westminster Abbey were covered with metal plates, yet they have been included in the above number, although these wooden cores cannot be called sculpture when deprived of their plates.

[6] Six Berkshire, four Buckinghamshire, one Brecknockshire, two Cambridgeshire, two Cumberland, two Derbyshire, two Devonshire, seven County Durham, ten Essex, two Gloucestershire, six Hampshire and the Isle of Wight, two Herefordshire, one Huntingdonshire, three Kent, two Middlesex, one Monmouthshire, one Nottinghamshire, three Norfolk, ten Northamptonshire, two Rutland, two Staffordshire, four Shropshire, two Somersetshire, six Suffolk, one Surrey, one Sussex, one Wiltshire, and nine Yorkshire.

[7] Six Brecknockshire, one Cumberland, one Devonshire, one County Durham, five Essex, one Herefordshire, one Hertfordshire, one Lincolnshire, two Nottinghamshire, one Northamptonshire, one Shropshire, and two Suffolk.

earl; seven were ladies, including one countess; and there was one bishop, one secular priest, one civilian, and one hermit.

The story of the destruction of these effigies is a painful episode in the history of monumental tombs. It is recorded by Major Davies that in the middle of the last century the washerwomen of Brecon were using fragments of the wooden effigy of Reginald Breos. Five out of six effigies belonging to the family of Games were destroyed by the Parliamentarian soldiers when they visited the priory church of Brecon. The effigy of Anthony, the last Lord Lucy of Egremont, Cumberland, disappeared about the close of the eighteenth century. The effigy of the wife of Sir John Stowford no longer exists at West Down, Devon, and the effigy which is supposed to have been that of Andrew Stanley, first Master of Greatham Hospital, County Durham, was existing in 1794. As many as four wooden effigies, probably belonging to the Vere family, and including at least one to an Earl of Oxford, were destroyed at Earl's Colne, Essex, during the third quarter of the eighteenth century. The effigy of Sir William Messing was actually ordered to be destroyed by the vicar of the church at Messing, Essex, about one hundred years ago, and the parish clerk obeyed the directions of his tactless superior to the very letter. An effigy in Abbey Dore is stated to have been that of Bishop Cadwgan, and in excellent preservation in 1716, as shown in a rough sketch given in the *Hill Manuscript*, reproduced by Mr. George Marshall, F.S.A., in his paper on "The Wooden Monumental Effigies of [1] Herefordshire," and where good reasons are adduced for believing that this effigy was removed from Abbey Dore between the years 1731 and 1769, although Gough declared it was in excellent preservation in 1786. Since that date it has been destroyed. The bishop died in 1225, and a wooden effigy of so

[1] See *Abbey Dore* in " Topographical Index " at end of this volume, where a résumé of Mr. Marshall's paper is given.

early a date would have been of great value. A diminutive effigy of a knight at Ayot St. Lawrence, Hertfordshire, has been destroyed, and one to Sir Baldwin Wake (died 1282) at Market Deeping, Lincolnshire, is no longer existing. An effigy of a knight, said to be Stephen Radcliffe, founder of the church at Radcliffe-on-Trent, Nottinghamshire, was removed from the church at the rejoicings that took place on the death of Tom Paine and burnt in a blazing bonfire. In 1818 an old hermitage in the west face of the Standard Hill rock, Nottingham, was cleared out and a grave containing human remains and a decayed wooden effigy was found. Until the early part of the eighteenth century the church of Holdenby, Northamptonshire, possessed a valuable wooden effigy of a franklin of the time of Edward III, and there is a tradition that it was removed by some gentleman who drove away with it in a carriage. Mr. Albert Hartshorne possessed a sketch of a wooden effigy of a knight of the Ercall family which once existed at High Ercall, Shropshire. This sketch was made by the late Rev. C. H. Hartshorne in 1835, and since that date the effigy has disappeared. Heveningham Church, Suffolk, has lost two wooden effigies; they were existing in 1833, but soon after that date they were wantonly destroyed by fire. This is only a meagre record, but there must have been, at one time, a vast number of wooden effigies which are now lost, or were even actually destroyed by their custodians or with their permission.

The exposure of the dead at the funeral was followed toward the close of the fourteenth century by the practice of bearing in the funeral procession the hastily made "lively effigy" of the dead person "in his very robes of estate." This was placed temporarily in the church under or associated with the "herse." These "lively figures" were closely allied to wooden effigies, and may have been suggested by them as their foundations were of wood, while the face and hands were of

B

wax or fine plaster tinted to life. These figures, dressed in gorgeous robes and with tinsel crowns and ornaments, presented a life-like appearance. Some of them, dating from Plantagenet times to the beginning of last century, are still preserved in Westminster Abbey, and are known as the "ragged Regiment."[1]

In Cornwallis's *Life of Prince Henry*, who died in 1612 at the age of eighteen, it is stated that the day before the funeral "his Representation was brought (made in so short Warning, as like him as could be) and apparelled with Cloaths, having his Creation Robes above the same, his Cap and Crown upon his Head, his Garter, Coller, with a *George* about his Neck, his golden Staff in his Right Hand lying cross a little; briefly, every Thing as he was apparelled at the Time of the Creation; which being done, it was laid on the Back on the Coffin, and fast bound to the same, the Head thereof being supported by two Cushions, just as it was to be drawn along the Streets in the Funeral Chariot."[2]

"The Coffin with the Representation (as is before said) remaining still under the Hearse, to be seen of all, until the 19th of the said Month of *December*,[3] when decked and trimmed with Cloaths, as he went when he was alive, Robes, Collar, Crown, Golden Rod in his Hand, &c., it was set up in a Chamber of the said Chapel at *Westminster*, amongst the Representations of the Kings and Queens, his famous Predecessors, where it remaineth for ever to be seen."[4]

We learn from a record in the reign of Henry III that

---

[1] See the exhaustive paper "On the Funeral Effigies of the Kings and Queens of England, with special reference to those in the Abbey Church of Westminster," by W. H. St. John Hope, in *Archæologia*, LX, 517–70 ; also *Some Minor Arts*, 57 ; *Portraiture in Recumbent Effigies*, by Albert Hartshorne, 28–30.

[2] Sir Charles Cornwallis, *An Account of the Baptism, Life, Death and Funeral of the Most Incomparable Prince Frederick Henry, Prince of Wales* (London, 1751), 47.

[3] Twelve days after the funeral.

[4] *Ibid.*, 50.

PLATE III.

Fig. 5.

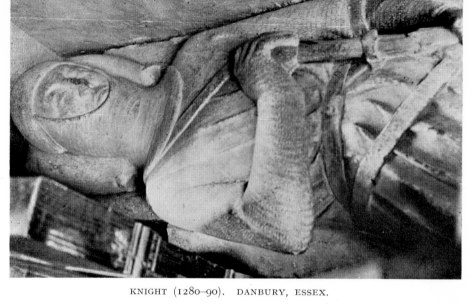

KNIGHT (1280–90). DANBURY, ESSEX.

Fig. 6.

TWO HORKSLEY KNIGHTS (*c.* 1290). LITTLE HORKSLEY, ESSEX.

Fig. 7.

? WIFE OF WILLIAM HORKSLEY (DIED 1296). LITTLE HORKSLEY, ESSEX.

wood was used for the foundation of a statue for the tomb of Princess Catherine, who died in 1257, which was covered with silver-gilt plates.[1] It is probable that this was for a figure of St. Catherine and not for an effigy of the princess. However, in 1296 we find that a tomb was erected in Westminster Abbey to William of Valence. This has a full-sized wooden figure covered with a number of plates of copper, some of which were enamelled. This work, like the tomb of Walter of Merton, Bishop of Rochester,[2] now destroyed, was sent from Limoges, and was doubtless the work of John of that city. The human form is poorly expressed, and the makeshift way of covering the junctions of the sheets with strips of filagree-work is poor art. The artist has depicted " banded mail," and the delicate enamel-work of a series of escutcheons on the surcoat, and the great enamelled shield worn on the hip after the French manner, show technical skill of a high order. This monument must have presented an appearance of great splendour when the wooden chest[3] upon which the effigy rests was also adorned with metal plates. These have all been removed, and this denuded memorial is but a shadow of a tomb which once presented a gorgeous and almost barbaric magnificence. The effigy of Henry V is also a wooden figure which was once adorned with silver plates. Queen Catherine, widow of Henry V, presented the effigy, but in 1546 thieves broke into the abbey,

[1] The Chancellor's Roll of 56 Henry III (1272).

[2] In the Louvre is a wooden effigy of Blanche de Champagne, died 1283. This is covered with plates of copper, and the head rests upon an enamelled cushion of Limoges work.

[3] An early example of a wooden tomb, but supporting a stone effigy, is that of William Longespée in Salisbury Cathedral church. The wooden tomb-chest under the effigy of Sir John Pitchford (1285) (Plate II) is an interesting example of thirteenth-century decoration, while the one under the effigy to Robert, Duke of Normandy, in Gloucester Cathedral (Plate I) is late fourteenth- or early fifteenth-century craftsmanship. The top of a fifteenth-century tomb-chest still remains at Brancepeth, and sixteenth-century ones are found at Burford, Derby, Thornhill, Staindrop, and Worsborough.

stripped the monument of its metal plates, and carried away the silver head of the king.[1]

The medieval artist selected a piece of oak, sound at the heart, in good condition, and sufficiently wide for him to carve the figure of a knight in armour or a lady in kirtle and long mantle lying on a board or bed. The portion of the board with the effigy on it, as well as the cushions upon which the head rested, and the animal at the feet, were hollowed out and filled with charcoal to absorb moisture.[2] Having carved the figure and fastened with wooden pins such parts as lay beyond the size of his block it was ready for decoration. The effigy would then be sized and pieces of linen would be glued over the cracks and other inequalities. The decorator would then give the figure a thin coat of so-called gesso, with a still thicker coating for those portions he desired to decorate in relief, such as the mail or surfaces afterwards to be gilded or silvered. Before the gesso hardened the decorator impressed it with various matrices or stamps of diverse patterns: some being for mail of various sizes and others for decorative purposes. Several processes were in use for gilding those surfaces required to be treated in this manner. To give depth or richness to the gold or silver leaf, they were first treated with bole Armenian[3] applied with white of egg either left dead or burnished with an agate. All the painting on the effigy was done in distemper (tempera). Finally the figure was covered with a coat of plain or tinted oleaginous varnish, which was

---

[1] The will of Henry VII expressed the desire that an " ymage of tymber " of a king, covered with plates of fine gold, in the manner of an armed man, be made and set up on the crest of the shrine of the Confessor.

[2] Blomefield found that the effigy of Sir Robert du Bois, who died 1311, was hollowed out and filled with charcoal.

[3] *The Bole Armenian* is an earthy mineral which occurs in amorphous masses and is composed chiefly of silica with 20 per cent of alumina and 10 of iron. It has a dull yellow, brownish, or red colour, has a greasy feel, and yields to the nail. It is opaque and slightly translucent.

needful, but, alas! it did not prove to be a sufficient protection.[1]

Great care and thought was always bestowed on the decoration of medieval effigies so that they glowed in colour and gleamed with gold leaf. The tints adopted were of the purest and brightest obtainable; for example, coloured grounds would be powdered with gold or white devices, yet exceptions to the heraldic rule of placing colour on colour and metal on metal are occasionally met with. For example, black patterns are sometimes depicted on green or red grounds, and in a few instances gold devices are found on white surfaces. These are, however, rare exceptions against the well-known rule of heraldry which was adopted generally, and, of course, the armorial bearings are correctly displayed on shield and surcoat, jupon and tabard, and on the lady's heraldic mantle. Red, blue, green, and white, and a sparing use of black, are found most frequently in use, and they are arranged so that they never clash, and by the avoidance of large surfaces of any one tint a beautiful colour scheme is obtained which is always harmonious and never gaudy.

Hollis gives a fine illustration of the Englefield lady, depicting her in a blue gown and mantle lined with red, the cushion upon which her head rests being a chocolate colour pricked out with a white pattern.[2] Traces of red may be seen on the arm of the later of the two knights (c. 1330) at Clifton Reynes, and his lady has evidently had a red kirtle with tight-fitting sleeves. In the deep folds of the surcoat of Sir John Hastings at Abergavenny we find fragments of a bright red; while Hawise Keynes, at Dodford, has a white wimple and a blue kirtle. Minute fragments of the decoration of the mantle of Dame Eleanor Treylli, at Woodford, show that "it was diapered in two shades of red and white in alternate quatrefoils containing

---

[1] Mr. Albert Hartshorne gives a detailed description of the use of gesso in the decoration of both stone and wooden effigies. See *Some Minor Arts*, 62–4.

[2] Hollis's *Monumental Effigies*.

concentric foliations and circles intermittently decorated with swans and cinquefoils."[1] The Rev. T. Kerrich has left us a faithful description of the colour he found on the effigy of a knight at Banham,[2] which has now, alas! been painted and sanded to represent stone. The surcoat was a brownish crimson flowered with yellow, the laces for the headpiece were red, the sword-belt and girdle yellow, flowered with green, and the spur-straps decorated with green, yellow, red, and black. The cushion under the head of the knight was black, flowered like the girdle, and the board was green, with flowers and leaves painted upon it. The links of mail were painted on a flat surface, but later in the fourteenth century they were frequently gilt.

Some decorations in gesso on stone effigies were designs exhibiting great variety and beauty, and Mr. Albert Hartshorne pointed out, in his valuable article on *Some Minor Arts*,[3] that many of the early ones were clearly inspired by oriental fabrics brought back by the Crusaders. Few of these beautiful designs are now to be seen on the wooden effigies, as only fragments of the ancient adornment have come down to us. The effigy of Sir Robert du Bois, at Fersfield, Norfolk, was repainted by Blomefield (1734) in the colours he found upon it. The head-piece, surcoat and gauntlets were powdered with ermine, and the girdle was coloured red inside. Fine patterns were worked in slight relief on sunk panels imitating enamels and placed on the gilded or silvered surfaces of the sword-belt and spur-straps, and also let into the board, which was green and adorned with flowers and leaves. Other effigies have been repainted in recent years, but it is impossible to know if those who carried out the work were as careful to retain the same colours as was the

[1] *Victoria History*, Northants, I, 401.
[2] See Gough's *Sepulchral Monuments*, I, Part i, 38 ; and the Kerrich Coll. (British Museum), 6732, p. 13.
[3] Page 63.

PLATE IV.

Fig. 8.

ARCHBISHOP PECKHAM (DIED 1292). CANTERBURY CATHEDRAL.

Fig. 9.

ARCHBISHOP PECKHAM (DIED 1292). CANTERBURY CATHEDRAL.

To face page 23.

restorer of the Fersfield figure. The effigy and cadaver at Worsborough were repainted in 1833 by a local man at Barnsley, and seven years later the one of John Heath, of Kepier, at St. Giles', Durham, was also repainted in colour ; while those at Brading, Burford, Chew Magna, Gloucester Cathedral Church, and Goudhurst have been similarly treated during the past sixty years.

Local legends have gathered round some of these dark and battered memorials of the dead. The effigy of the knight at Berrington has long been known as *Old Scriven*, and he is reputed to have been a great warrior who slew a lion at Eaton Mascot. The lion, however, gave the knight a fearful wound in the face before it was dispatched by his good sword. No doubt the lion at the foot of the effigy and the damaged face of the knight were the groundwork of a story which is widely circulated. For long the effigy at Chew Magna [1] has been called Sir John Hauteville, whose gigantic strength was reputed to be such that he was able to throw two stone quoits, each weighing upwards of 30 tons, the distance of a mile, and to have carried three men to the top of Norton church tower, one under each arm and the third in his teeth. The position of the effigy of a knight at Bures may have given colour to the story that this man in a drunken freak sold his property of Corn Hall for fourpence. Whereupon the clergy declared he should neither be buried in the church nor in the churchyard. Hence he received burial in the wall. The dilapidated fragment of a knight at Midsomer Norton is commonly called Jack O'Lent, and the spurious thirteenth-century effigy at Gatcombe is known as St. Radegund, although the effigy is that of a man, and the saint was a queen. Vast numbers of Yorkshire people

---

[1] This curious effigy is probably to John Wych. The Manor of Norton passed into his possession in 1328, and this effigy was most likely carved before 1350, as he died in 1346.

annually visit the effigy of Sir Thomas Cresacre at Barnborough on account of an ancient story which asserts that he was attacked by a wild cat, and there was a running fight until they reached the porch of the church, where the mortal combat ended in the death of both. It may be that there is some truth in the story, and that the knight was attacked by one of these ferocious animals, or it may have originated from the crest of this family being a catamountain, or even from some red-coloured stones in the porch which tradition declares to be the spot where the conflict ended.

PLATE V.

Fig. 10.

SECOND DANBURY KNIGHT (*c.* 1300).   DANBURY, ESSEX.

Fig. 11.

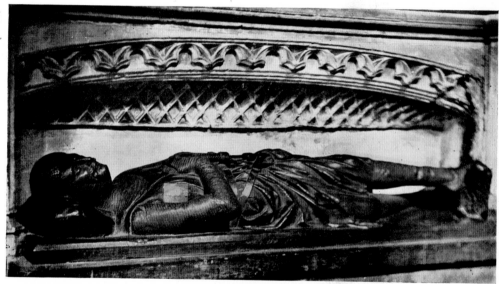

KNIGHT (RESTORED) (1290–1300)   SOUTHWARK CATHEDRAL.

Fig. 12.

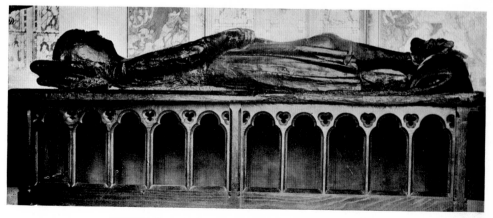

KNIGHT (*c.* 1300).   HILDERSHAM, CAMBRIDGESHIRE.

PART II

EARLIER WOODEN EFFIGIES TO THE BLACK DEATH

(1280–1350)

TWO of the earlier wooden effigies possess histories which it is necessary to recall. The first refers to the effigy of Robert, Duke of Normandy, in Gloucester Cathedral Church.[1] The duke died in 1135, and it is now considered that the effigy was probably made about the year 1280. Canon Bazeley points out [2] that the figure is very similar to the effigy of Richard, Earl of Cornwall, who died in 1272, found at Hayles Abbey, if we can judge from the fragments. The crown on Duke Robert's effigy, with its fleurs-de-lys and strawberry leaves, is similar to that introduced by Henry IV; it has no arch or crosses patée such as appear in later royal crowns. During the Civil War the effigy was broken in pieces and sold to Sir Humphrey Tracey, of Stanway, who kept it until the Restoration, when it was mended and again placed in the cathedral. It is difficult to know how much of the present effigy is original, and which portions were added at the Restoration to make good any fragments that were missing. If, however, a new crown had been constructed it would

[1] The effigy rests on an oblong wooden box of late fourteenth- or early fifteenth-century workmanship, and now lies in the presbytery. It seems that the body of the duke was removed into the presbytery after the suppression of the abbey, as the inscription "Hic jacet Robertus Curtus" is in the chapter-house.

[2] See *Transactions of the Bristol and Gloucestershire Archæological Society*, XXVII, 289.

have had eight strawberry leaves only. The effigy appears to be solid, and the hauberk, with its continuous hood and other details, indicates its early character. The thickness of the paint with which it was covered in the reign of Charles II makes it impossible to say by what method the mail is represented. This effigy was made, probably, in Bristol, and is considered by some authorities to be one of the oldest existing wooden effigies we now possess, and is a memorial of a forlorn captive who is such a pathetic character in the history of England.

The second effigy is a knight in St. Saviour's Cathedral Church, Southwark, which has been "restored," and Mr. Albert Hartshorne conjectures that the restorer was probably Richardson, who was busy doing similar work on the Temple effigies some seventy years ago. The restorer appears to have coated the effigy with some sort of dark gesso, and then impressed all over the mail with a tool. Originally it was, doubtless, an excellent effigy, but it is now very difficult to know the full extent of the "restoration," and it is probable that the restorer considerably changed the appearance of the figure. The face is evidently modern with protruding eyes and hooked nose. There should have been no moustache like the one depicted, as the face would have been clean-shaven; and the hood should have covered most of the chin to form a protection. As the hands are in mufflers we should expect the hood of mail and the hauberk to be continuous, but this is not the case, and the head is in a coif of mail. This shows a serious anachronism. The original effigy was doubtless carved between 1290 and 1300; and when the restorer took it in hand he probably found a denuded, decaying wooden figure, but he has improved it, particularly in the loose lie of the mail and the folds of the surcoat.

Now that we have considered the "restoration" of the Southwark knight, we must turn our attention to the wooden cross-legged effigy of a knight placed in a recess in the north wall of Gatcombe Church which has long been an antiquarian puzzle.

Some have conjectured that it is an early figure of a knight in mail, with surcoat, sword, and shield, which has suffered much from many reckless and ill-advised restorations. Others, however, like Mr. Percy G. Stone, F.S.A.,[1] have come to the conclusion that it is an anachronism which was perpetrated in Jacobean times. Such things were very frequently done, and Mr. Stone reminds us that this was especially the case with the effigies of ancestors made by minor artists. This effigy is certainly the work of an inferior sculptor and possesses little merit, and cannot even be considered quaint. The head is encased in a salade which is certainly not of the thirteenth century, but there is no doubt that the head of the knight and the angel supporting the cushion are more recent restorations. The only part of the mail which may be ancient is the hauberk, and the portion below the waist is not likely to be earlier than the fifteenth century, while the consensus of opinion declares that it has a Jacobean feeling. If the effigy were intended to represent some member of the Estur family, to whom the manor of Gatcombe belonged from the time of Domesday until the reign of Edward II, the shield would have been kite-shaped had it been carved before the middle of the thirteenth century, and if the figure had been executed later than that date the circular cushion under the head would have been replaced by two cushions, the upper one lozenge-shaped and the lower one rectangular ; and in any case the shield-strap is too broad.

The series of wooden effigies contains only one of a lawyer. This is to be found at West Down, Devon, and represents Sir John Stowford, who died about 1372. He was a judge in the Court of Common Pleas, and for one month (November, 1345) was Chief Baron of the Exchequer. His effigy is fully robed. The under gown or cassock reaches to his feet, and the tight-

[1] See Percy G. Stone, *Architectural Antiquities of the Isle of Wight*, II, 25.

fitting sleeves can be seen under the outer gown. The tippet is pleated at the shoulders, and is evidently made of a softer material than those of the time of Henry VI. The hood falls forward on the neck, and the head was doubtless in a coif, but it is now sadly mutilated.

Although we have only one lawyer, yet the church is represented by five ecclesiastics. The oldest effigy is that of a priest at Clifford, Herefordshire. It is a particularly fine and perfect wooden figure, probably representing a rector of this parish about the year 1280. He is tonsured and robed in Eucharistic vestments, and the long chasuble (3 feet 10 inches) is depicted in elegant folds. This chasuble, however, has not the multitudinous folds, nor is it so pointed, as those found on effigies of bishops and priests dating from 1225–1250; neither is it as full and heavy in the folds as those shown on effigies of 1290–1300. The length of the chasuble and the treatment of the folds are very similar to the chasubles depicted on the effigies of Bishop Aquablanca of Hereford, who died 1268, and Bishop Bronescombe, of Exeter, who died in 1280. The treatment of the hair on the Clifford priest is very similar to these Hereford and Exeter bishops. It is not impossible that the face is a portrait. The nose is damaged, the eyes are open, and the features show considerable character. This oak figure resembles the drapery and pose of the effigy of Bishop Aquablanca in Hereford Cathedral, and it seems not unlikely that an imager of Hereford carved it some years before the close of the thirteenth century.

The effigy of Archbishop Peckham, who died in 1296, rests on the original tomb in the north wall of the Martyrdom of Canterbury Cathedral Church. He is vested in alb, amice, stole, tunicle, dalmatic, chasuble, pall, mitre, and gloves, and when this figure was painted it must have presented an appearance as rich and magnificent as the stone effigy of Bishop Brones-

PLATE VI.

Fig. 13.

LADY (*c.* 1300). HILDERSHAM, CAMBRIDGESHIRE.

Fig. 14.

KNIGHT (*c.* 1310). MONKS SHERBORNE PRIORY, HAMPSHIRE.

Fig. 15.

SIR PHILIP LE LOU (*c.* 1315). ASHTON, NORTHANTS.

To face page 29.

combe (1280) in Exeter Cathedral Church. The mitre appears to have been made separately and may, possibly, have been constructed of metal or enamelled copper plates. Although in 1290 King Henry III and Queen Eleanor were commemorated in bronze, and marble was still largely used for the memorials of great personages, yet wood was selected for an effigy of an archbishop of Canterbury, on which the decorator's skill would be expended in painted patterns with gilding and jewels. In attitude and drapery this oak figure is so similar to the " Lady Aveline " in Westminster Abbey that it was, probably, made in a London workshop.

The third effigy of an ecclesiastic is met with at Little Leighs, Essex, and reposes under a beautiful ogee arch of the same date. This effigy is also robed in Eucharistic vestments and probably dates from about the year 1320. The authors of *Medieval Figure Sculpture in England* [1] consider that it is copied from the stone " Ancaster " type of figure which is a rough title that is given for effigies made from the Rutland and Lincolnshire oolites.

Our fourth effigy of an ecclesiastic is in All Saints' Church, Derby. This figure represents a secular canon vested in cassock, surplice, almuce, and cope. Sir William Hope, in his paper on this effigy,[2] points out that it shows most admirably the tails forming the fringe of the furred almuce, and those on the pendant in front. The addition of the cope is an uncommon feature. It is conjectured with great probability that this is the effigy of Robert Johnson, who was sub-dean of the collegiate church of All Saints', Derby, as late as 1527. He was a great benefactor to this church. In 1723 All Saints' Church

---

[1] Page 662.

[2] *Journal of the Derbyshire Archæological and Natural History Society*, XIII, 185–9. The effigy and cadaver were exhibited by Sir William Hope to the Society of Antiquaries on the 13th March 1884. See *Proceedings*, 2nd S., X, 63–6, and the accompanying engraving of the sub-dean's effigy.

was demolished except the tower, and this tomb was broken up. The south side was preserved on account of its elaborate carving, while the effigy and cadaver found a home in a damp vault. Sir William Hope obtained the help of the Derbyshire Archæological and Natural History Society in 1879, and after some delay the work of restoration was proceeded with. The head of the effigy, which was loose, had been stolen before the figure was removed from the vault. Sir William Hope was fortunately able to recover it. The side of the tomb had been affixed to the consistory seat. It was removed in 1885 and became the south side of the monument. This fine piece of carving has thirteen figures of bedefolk sculptured in high relief, and they stand in an arcade with singular pointed canopies supported by twisted shafts.

The church of Steeple Langford contains a wooden effigy to the Rev. Joseph Collier, who was rector from 1607 to 1635. It is a half-figure now placed in a niche over the vestry door, but it stood formerly against the south wall of the nave in an elaborate frame. The figure is painted, and the reverend gentleman is portrayed in cassock with girdle, collar and cuffs as worn by the clergy of that date, and a black skull-cap covers the top of his head. The hands are clasped over a small red volume.

Although there are five ecclesiastics, yet we find only three laymen in the series of wooden effigies. They are franklins, and date from about the middle of the fourteenth century.[1] The one at Eaton-under-Heywood, Shropshire, reposes under a beautiful cinquefoiled canopy, decorated with the scroll moulding and adorned with the ball-flower. He is dressed in a long cote which conceals the inner garment, and the close-fitting hood covers the head. The other effigy is at Much Marcle,

---

[1] Mr. Bloxam dates the one at Much Marcle about 1350, and Mr. Albert Hartshorne would assign it to about the year 1360.

Herefordshire, and the figure has a close-fitting cote-hardie, buttoned in front, reaching to the knees, and possessing tight-fitting sleeves buttoned from the elbows to the wrists. The hood is worn about the neck and part of the breast, but is not drawn over the head. Over the hips is a leathern girdle with a long pendant, and a small purse is buckled to it. The legs are in close-fitting hose, the right is crossed over the left, and the shoes are pointed. Cross-legged effigies in the dress of a civilian are very rare. Mr. Bloxam points out [1] that there is one in Thurlaston Church, Leicestershire, and one at Birkin, near Normanton. Mr. George Marshall, F.S.A., in his paper on *Wooden Monumental Effigies in Herefordshire*, points out that Walter de Helyon had come into full possession of the Marcle property in 1348, when it was made over to his only child Joan. He was alive in 1357 and probably died soon afterwards. This date comes very near to the year 1360, which was the date Mr. Albert Hartshorne assigned to this effigy. Walter de Helyon was a man of wealth and property, and it is, therefore, not unlikely that his only child should have erected this memorial to his memory, and it may be compared with the early alabaster tables, which may be dated about 1350. These tables were made at Nottingham, and an example is now in the Carcassonne Museum. "The correspondence bears out the view," Prof. Prior and Mr. Gardner remark, "that in these cases we have an imager's shop supplying effigies with the help of patterns current in stone sculpture." [2] The sprawling lion at the feet of the effigy and the square cushion with its tasselled corners indicate that this figure emanated from the hand of a Hereford imager about the middle of the fourteenth century.

At Little Baddow, Essex, are two effigies in wood; one is

[1] *Archæological Journal*, XXXIII, 239.
[2] *Medieval Figure Sculpture in England*, 663. See Fig. 546, of alabaster tables in Carcassonne Museum.

a lady dressed in sleeveless cote-hardie, kirtle, wimple, and veil, and the other is doubtless her husband in the dress of a civilian. He wears an under tunic or cassock with tight-fitting sleeves fastened with eighteen buttons, and his outer cote has wide open sleeves reaching only to the elbows. The hair is worn long, falling in curls to the neck, and the face is clean-shaven. Mr. Chancellor, in his *Sepulchral Monuments of Essex*,[1] considers that the effigies represent mother and daughter rather than two sisters as the tradition runs. The long gown and the hair worn in wavy ringlets to the shoulders evidently deceived Mr. Chancellor when he classed this effigy as a lady belonging to the first half of the fourteenth century.

The question of portraiture in effigies is one which the late Mr. Albert Hartshorne made his own,[2] and after studying his valuable book we feel sure that some few of the wooden effigies belonging to the thirteenth and fourteenth centuries may have been portraits, as they exhibit a marked variety of countenances, and one or two even portray individuality and character. The five ecclesiastics might well have been executed from life or even produced from careful instructions given after death. Yet, in many instances, the faces we now look upon must have been caricatures of the men and women they pretend to represent. Surely William of Valence in Westminster Abbey never possessed so crude a countenance as John of Limoges has given him; while the features of Sir Thomas Cresacre at Barnborough and John Hastings at Abergavenny may well have been intended for portraits. In fact protraiture was carried out only where circumstances were favourable for its production. In some cases the effigies were made during lifetime, and in others perhaps from sketches made by those who remembered the deceased; while in the later part of the fourteenth century

[1] Note to Plate CXXV.
[2] *Portraiture in Recumbent Effigies*, by Albert Hartshorne.

PLATE VII.

Fig. 16.

Fig. 17.

KNIGHT (1305–10). WHORLTON, YORKS.

KNIGHT (*c.* 1310). BURGHFIELD, BERKS.

and throughout the two following centuries no doubt in special cases the artist availed himself of the likeness in wax or fine plaster of the "living" figure of the deceased borne on the "herse" in the funeral procession.

It seems more than probable that many of the early wooden effigies came from workshops where the image-makers had full appliances for producing them artistically. They were highly finished productions, and London, Bristol, and Hereford had each its speciality in effigies. There is a peculiarity in the representation of the mail upon the arms of the hauberk, as this is carved in stone and marble at Salisbury, Wareham, Shepton Mallet, and Malvern, and other places as well as in the statues at Wells, and in the wooden effigy of Robert, Duke of Normandy, at Gloucester. Since this peculiarity is particularly to be observed in the knights at Bristol, which were carved, say, from 1250 to 1280, it may be conjectured that a school for the production of stone effigies established itself at Bristol, and that in copy of these Robert, Duke of Normandy, was made. Some few wooden effigies, however, appear to be the work of unskilled carvers, and the ill-shaped figure of Sir Thomas le Latimer, at Braybrooke, Northamptonshire, was possibly the product of a village Phidias in the year 1334. It is unfortunate that the painting has all disappeared, as it would have been interesting to see how the village decorator covered this particularly gnarled and knotty piece of oak with his gesso work. The same may be said of the "knight" at Auckland, County Durham, and the civilian and lady at Little Baddow in Essex, where we find a local effort in copying stone effigies and probably of some others. It is not likely that the military effigies of knights with legs crossed and legs straight emanated from the same workshops at the same time ; nor were the effigies of knights with hands raised on the breast in the attitude of prayer and those holding their sword-hilts

c

executed by the same carver; nor the ladies with looped-up skirts from the same workshop as the dames in long mantles.

Although a vast number of wooden effigies have been ruthlessly destroyed, yet fortunately we still possess a sufficient number to enable us to trace the progress of English effigies in wood from the latter part of the thirteenth century, when the figure of Robert, Duke of Normandy, was placed in St. Peter's Abbey at Gloucester, to the middle of the seventeenth century, when that of Sir John Oglander was carved for Brading Church.

The group of wooden effigies made in the thirteenth century is not large. We have already referred to those of Robert, Duke of Normandy, and the knight in St. Saviour's Cathedral Church, Southwark, and have dwelt on their vicissitudes and the " restorations " they have passed through. Sir John Pitchford died in 1285, and his wooden effigy rests on an oblong chest in the chancel of St. Michael's Church at Pitchford. This is a very fine effigy, and one of the earliest we now possess. In several respects the knight resembles the stone effigy of William Longespée in Salisbury Cathedral Church, a little earlier in date, but also resting on a wooden tomb. It is probable that the sculptors of both effigies were influenced by the same school of carving. The length and shape of the surcoat, the flat-topped hood, and the buckling on the sword-belt indicate that the effigy of Sir John Pitchford was probably executed during the later years of the thirteenth century. The wooden tomb decorated with trefoil-headed arches, each containing a heater-shaped shield of arms suspended by a strap, is very remarkable. Another wooden effigy of this century is to Margaret, second wife of Adam of Everingham, at Laxton, Nottinghamshire. This is a graceful figure of a lady in a wimple, veil flowing to the shoulders and confined round the head with a circlet, a kirtle, and a mantle caught up under her arm.

PLATE VIII.

Fig. 18.

SIR RALPH REYNES (*c.* 1310) AND WIFE.   CLIFTON REYNES, BUCKINGHAMSHIRE.

Fig. 19.

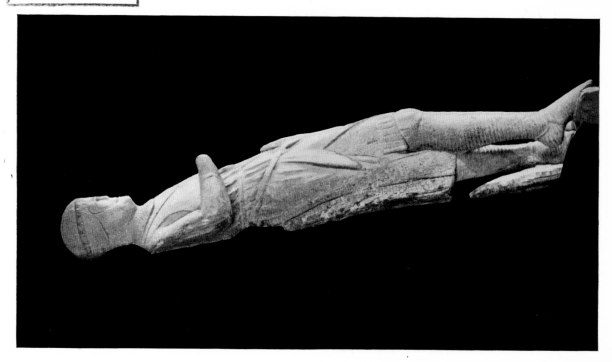

KNIGHT (*c.* 1310–20).   OUSBY, CUMBERLAND.

This effigy and the stone effigies to her husband and his first wife are all crowded together on the founder's tomb, so that the wooden figure projects over the side of the slab, and, in fact, the canopy was destroyed to make room for them. Some suppose that this was done when the wooden effigy was made, but others surmise that it took place at a later date when the south chapel was so inconveniently crowded with tombs that these three effigies were removed to the position they now occupy. The beautiful effigy of a priest at Clifford, Herefordshire (*c.* 1280), the restored "knight" in St. Saviour's Cathedral Church, Southwark (1290–1300), and the fine memorial to Archbishop Peckham, who died in 1292, belong to this century, and we must also assign some date in the closing years of the thirteenth century to the two wooden effigies at Little Horkesley, Essex. The lady is in a costume very similar to that of Margaret of Everingham at Laxton, save that her mantle is shorter. She may be the wife of Sir William Horkesley, who died in 1296. The knight is probably a member of the Horkesley family, and may be Sir William Horkesley. The hoods of both the Horkesley knights are concentrically ringed round the face, and this indicates an early fashion, while the surcoat of the shorter knight is open up to the waist like the effigy of Robert, Duke of Normandy, in Gloucester Cathedral Church, to which we assign 1280 as not altogether an impossible date. Another early effigy, and possibly belonging to this century, is the oldest of the three knights at Danbury, in Essex.

The figure of the knight in mail at Berrington, Shropshire, is well carved, and so are the three knights of the great Clare family at Danbury, Essex.[1] The fine and reposeful figure of a knight at Monks Sherborne Priory, Hampshire, has been ascribed, quite erroneously, to Sir John Port or Porz, but must be of some other knight half a century after his time.

[1] One is much later than the other two.

All these fine and skilfully executed figures show us with what care and conscientiousness the old sculptors in wood finished their work, which was immediately coated over and painted.

The effigy in mail of a knight at Clifton Reynes, Buckinghamshire, which has been known as Sir Simon Borard for many years, must be dated about 1310, and is probably that of Sir Ralph Reynes, who died in that year. At Ousby in Cumberland we find an effigy of a knight which must have been carved between 1310 and 1320, and the artist has not set out the mail on the hauberk regularly, although he has depicted the mail on the hose in regular and parallel lines. The camail is attached to a bascinet decorated with a lozenge pattern by means of loops and laces not now visible. At Elmstead, Essex, we find a knight (1300–1315), who is probably one of the Tony family. He wears a helm over his coif of mail, and is an interesting transitional figure between the simple mail hood and the bascinet attached. The head of this knight rests on a lion, while his feet are placed in the lap of a civilian of the time of Edward II. This figure is in a long gown reaching to just below the ankles, and a hood, of which the long folds hang down the shoulders behind. The upper part of the figure has been so mutilated that some writers have come to the conclusion that it was intended for a woman. This, however, could not have been the case, as at that period the women never exposed their feet in the way we see in this figure.[1]

At Woodford, Northamptonshire, we find the wooden effigies of a knight and his wife, said to be Sir Walter Treylli and Dame Eleanor his wife, resting on a high tomb. The knight has a round head-piece on the coif of mail, or perhaps it is attached to it, and his knees are protected with poleyns of plate, the precursors of the more shapely knee-cops. The sword

[1] Professor Prior conjectures that the figure may have been an angel, similar to those at Westminster.

is suspended by two lockets in accordance with the new fashion then coming into use. There are no spurs, but this may doubtless be attributed to an oversight on the part of the artist of this excellent figure. The lady is also well proportioned. She wears a tight-sleeved kirtle, and a sleeveless cote-hardie, gathered up under the left arm in the usual way, falls in voluminous and graceful folds. Over this is worn a mantle; a deep wimple is fastened under the chin, and a long coverchief falls over it in many folds.[1]

The diaper work on this mantle has already been described, and is in two shades of red, with centres of white swans and "wrythen" foliations. It has been pointed out[2] that the general scheme is similar to that in the enamels on the pillow of William of Valence in Westminster Abbey. Sir John Treylli died in 1290, but the details of his armour show that the effigy is later, and it is therefore conjectured that his widow, Dame Eleanor, erected both memorials; she died in 1316.

The wooden effigy to Sir William Combmartin (1318) at Alderton, Northamptonshire, was banished to the belfry in 1848, but has again been placed in the church. Although the effigy has suffered seriously from damp, and is in a sad state of decay, yet it is a work of high artistic quality and exhibits a figure in an attitude of great repose. It has been demonstrated[3] that the loose fit of the mail and the straight under eyelid are features which are associated with wooden effigies of this, the best age, and are found in stone effigies of fully half a century earlier.[4]

The Alderton knight must be compared with the effigy to Sir John Hastings (1313) at Abergavenny, Monmouthshire. Mr.

[1] *Victoria History of Northants*, I, 401.
[2] *Some Minor Arts*, 59.
[3] *Some Minor Arts*, 64.
[4] These peculiarities appear in stone effigies before 1250, as at Wells and conspicuously at Westminster Abbey.

Octavius Morgan attributed this effigy to George Cantelupe, but he died in 1273, and this effigy belongs to the early years of the fourteenth century. Churchyard, who wrote in the beginning of Elizabeth's reign, states that the effigy then lay on a window-ledge

> . . . . removed away
> By fine device of man:
> And layd within a windowe right,
> Full flat on stonie wall:
> Where now he doth in open sight,
> Remain to people all.

But he is now removed from this elevated position and placed at the west end of the Herbert Chapel in St. Mary's Priory Church. The perfect dignity and repose of this effigy is finely conceived, and the whole design is grand in the extreme. Mr. Albert Hartshorne compares the wooden effigies at Alderton and Abergavenny with those in stone to Edmund, Earl of Lancaster, died 1296, and Aymer of Valence, died 1323, which are both in Westminster Abbey; and he is convinced that all four came from the same art centre, conjecturing that London was probably the workshop where they were fashioned. As John Hastings married as his first wife Isabel, sister to Aymer of Valence, it seems reasonable to consider that the same sculptor might have been employed to execute his monument as well as that of his brother-in-law.

Two wooden effigies of considerable interest are placed in the chancel of Weston-under-Lyzard Church, Staffordshire. The one in the north wall recess is probably to Sir John Weston. He accompanied the Princess Elizabeth, Countess of Holland and Hereford, as her attorney when she went into Flanders with her father, King Edward I. Sir John Weston had charge of the jewels which the princess took with her, and the little purse suspended to the belt may possibly represent his badge of

PLATE III.

PLATE IX.

Fig. 20.

SIR ROBERT DU BOIS (DIED 1311). FERSFIELD, NORFOLK.

Fig. 21.

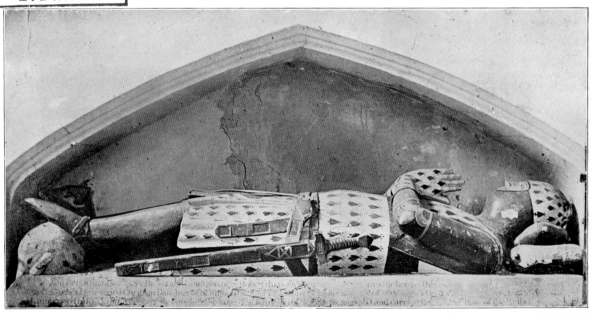

SIR ROBERT DU BOIS (DIED 1311). FERSFIELD, NORFOLK.

office. Such a purse is rarely appended to a military costume, but it is occasionally found on effigies to civilians. It is a curious fact that at High Ercall and at Leighton-under-Wrekin in the next county [1] are stone effigies having purses suspended in a similar manner and of like size and dimensions. It is quite possible that the imager or wood carver copied from the stone effigy at High Ercall,[2] for the mason and the imager would each have his own distinct establishment in all probability. However, it seems scarcely likely that a little purse would indicate a badge of office for all three knights. Sir John Weston most likely died soon after his return from Flanders, but the exact date of his death is not known; it was probably about 1304. His effigy is an interesting work of art and is better constructed than the one in the south wall recess, which is presumably that of his nephew, Sir Hugh Weston, who died in 1305. It is to be regretted that the modern inscription placed above these effigies is not accurate, as it states that one is to Sir Hamo Weston, who died in 1188, which is quite an impossible date to assign to any English wooden effigy.

At Whorlton, Yorkshire, we possess a fine effigy to a knight in mail (1305–1310). The feet of this figure appear as if they are uncovered and the toes are visible, yet, for all that, they are armed with spurs, and the straps still remain. It has been suggested by Sir William Hope that the feet were encased in thin leather, like gloves, as the spurs could hardly have been attached to bare ankles.

At Bures, Suffolk, is found an effigy of a knight in mail still possessing his shield. This defence was usually pinned on with wooden pegs and consequently easily lost. This knight is said to have been called Corne or Cornard.

---

[1] Shropshire.
[2] The stone effigy at High Ercall was carved some few years earlier than the one to Sir John Weston at Weston-under-Lyzard.

The wooden effigy of Sir Robert du Bois, who died in 1311 in his forty-fourth year, is at Fersfield, Norfolk. Blomefield, the historian, was rector of Fersfield, and he found sufficient remains of colour on this effigy for him to attempt repainting it in 1734 in the same colours and design. The head of this fine figure is in a coif of mail on which is a head-piece powdered with ermine. The scabbard and board had embellishments with devices which are now lost, but were separate attachments originally. This effigy is not cross-legged, and at the feet is a spotted buck, being the crest of Du Bois. Although Robert du Bois died in 1311, yet this effigy is an instance of the straight-legged attitude, and it is therefore possible that it was not executed until the middle of the fourteenth century,[1] when this peculiarity again made its appearance. The figure was most likely carved in London. The wooden effigies being hollowed out were comparatively light and therefore easy of transport, and one made in Bristol could as easily be sent to Gloucester as one fashioned in London could be dispatched in a packing-case to Fersfield.

On a modern table-tomb at Ashton, Northamptonshire, rests the dilapidated wooden effigy of Sir Philip le Lou (1315) in a melancholy state of decay, and the monument and wooden effigy in mail of Sir Philip Gayton, at Gayton in the same county, had also fallen into bad condition until it was well and judiciously restored in 1830.

In the north aisle of Banham Church, Norfolk, is an empty wall-recess wherein rested a wooden effigy for many centuries. For some strange reason the custodians have now removed it to a new wall-recess they have made for it in the chancel, and the authorities have also thought good to sand it over so that it may present the appearance of stone. The effigy as shown in Gough's illustration has peg-marks all over him, which cannot

---

[1] The apron-like appearance of the surcoat indicates the cyclas period.

PLATE X.

PLATE X.

Fig. 22.

? KNIGHT OF THE BERRINGTON FAMILY.   BERRINGTON, SHROPSHIRE.

Fig. 23.

BARON JOHN HASTINGS (DIED 1313).   PRIORY CHURCH, ABERGAVENNY, MONMOUTHSHIRE.

now be seen owing to many repaintings. It is conjectured that these were for attachments of metal as in William of Valence (1290), the bronze effigies of Richard II and Anne of Bohemia, and in Henry V's effigy. This latter figure had a foundation of wood finished with elaborate surface and accessories and furnished with plates of enamelled metal. Fortunately Mr. Kerrich has left us a record of the colours and designs he found upon it before this was done. The effigy belongs to the first half of the fourteenth century and cannot be earlier than 1310, and was, possibly, carved between 1340 and 1350. The knight is in mail, and over the coif of mail is a head-piece fastened by laces which are not now visible, and his short sleeveless surcoat reaches to just above the knees. Blomefield and Gough conjectured that this splendid effigy represented Sir Hugh Bardolph, who died in 1203; but they were quite mistaken, and it must have been more than a hundred years later when it was carved.

We find a fine effigy of a knight in mail at Burghfield, Berkshire. His left side has been completely destroyed, and he also wears a head-piece over his coif of mail. This fine figure, possessing all the characteristics of London craftsmanship of about the year 1310, appears to have served as a model for the earlier of the two stone knights at Warkworth, Northants, and for a much-worn effigy of a knight at Sparsholt, Berkshire. Lysons considered that the excellent effigy to a knight in mail at Hildersham, Cambridgeshire, was to Sir Thomas Busteler, but he died in 1370, and this effigy shows a knight who died some sixty years earlier. The knight in mail at Ashwell, Rutland, belongs to some member of the Touchet family. At Allerton Mauleverer, Yorkshire, we find two knights in mail, and the later of them has a head-piece strapped on to his coif of mail; while at Auckland, in the county of Durham, we find an effigy of a knight which has not emanated from the workshops of London, Hereford, or Bristol, but must have been of local construction. It is no work of high art, but the village craftsman has expended considerable care over the details. He portrays the knight, who is doubtless some member of the Pollard family, in a hauberk with sleeves prolonged to form mittens with thumb pieces. The mail of the hauberk and camail is well depicted, but the hose are smooth, and it is possible that the mail was painted on them, or they may be intended for jambarts of plate or boiled leather. The knight's head is in a bascinet with the camail attached, showing the lacings. The surcoat falls to the knees and is longer behind than in front.

The later of the two knights at Clifton Reynes, Buckinghamshire, was carved about 1330, and was probably some member of the Reynes family. The knight is in mail, and he wears a skull-cap under his coif of mail, and beneath the hauberk is his quilted gambeson. His surcoat does not reach to his knees by several inches, and has an embattled border. This short surcoat marks the period immediately preceding the appearance of the cyclas. The wooden effigy to Sir Thomas le Latimer (died 1334) at Braybrooke, Northamptonshire, is a remarkably proportioned figure, and like the effigy at Auckland was the work of a village carver. It is an ill-shaped figure, carved out of a piece of knotty oak, and is 7 feet 4 inches in length. The carver has shown Sir Thomas in a short surcoat scarcely reaching to the knees and slit at the sides.

About the year 1321 a new fashion began to make its appearance. The surcoat was found to be inconveniently long, and when knights were dismounted and obliged to fight on foot the ample folds became entangled in their legs. Thus a new and curious military garment was fashioned by cutting away the whole of the front of the surcoat up to the middle of the thighs, slitting up the sides to the hips, taking it in at the body and lacing it up on the right side. This was called the *cyclas*, and it appears to have been a peculiarly English garment, not having been met with on the Continent on either stone military effigies or on brasses. The total number of examples do not amount to a score.

Our series of wooden monumental effigies depicts two knights in the cyclas. The first is Sir Lawrence Pavely, at Paulespury, Northamptonshire, and here we find the cyclas portrayed with loose sleeves reaching below the elbows. The knight wears a conical and fluted bascinet of extremely rare occurrence, to which a camail is attached by laces running through loops,[1] a haketon with tight-fitting sleeves, plain cuffed gauntlets, and fluted knee-cops, while the feet are armed with rowel spurs, and the legs are clothed in mail hose bound with a cord below the knee. The sword is fastened by a double locket placed a few inches below the top of the scabbard. This monument dates about 1330, and shows a decline both in art and execution, although the figure of the knight's wife has considerable merit, and the gathered-up folds of her drapery show a fair amount of artistic power. The interest connected with the cyclas and the fluted bascinet worn by Sir Lawrence Pavely redeem his figure from being classed as in any way commonplace. These effigies lie upon a high freestone tomb. The north and south sides are adorned with uncharged shields suspended alternately from foliage and heads under ogeed canopies of good design, cusped and sub-cusped. At the west end are two plain shields : one is suspended from a queen's head crowned and wearing a wimple, the other from the head of a king bearded and crowned, and perhaps intended for Edward III.

We have to turn to Barnborough, in Yorkshire, to find our

---

[1] The brasses of Sir John Creke at Westley Waterless, and of Sir John d'Aubernoun at Stoke d'Abernon, both show the cyclas and also the fluted bascinet. These brasses are illustrated in Haines's *Monumental Brasses*, Part I, CLI, CLII.

second example of the cyclas. Here we find an effigy in wood of high artistic conception, and when we look at the well-executed face we wonder if it be an example of portraiture, and if this be a likeness of Sir Thomas Cresacre, who was living in 1344. The fashion of wearing a cyclas ended about 1346, so this is one of the later effigies showing this strange military garment,[1] and is an instance not given in the usual lists of brasses and effigies exhibiting the cyclas. The knight wears a bascinet, camail, gambeson (showing well the quilted and padded nature of the garment), articulated shoulder-pieces, vambraces, elbow-cops, brassarts, thigh-pieces, knee-cops, jambs, articulated sollerets, while the feet are armed with rowel spurs, and the hands are in gauntlets, being raised on the breast in the attitude of prayer and holding a heart between the open palms indicative of the pictorial prayer for mercy, or more probably indicating that the knight's heart was preserved in the church. A small wall recess still exists which may have been constructed for this purpose.

The fashion of wearing the cyclas only lasted a quarter of a century, and then the jupon made its appearance. The long flap behind the cyclas cut away, the lower edges were escalloped or fringed, and it was laced up at the side. The earliest effigies displaying the jupon are about 1340, and the fashion lasted until the end of the century and the early years of the next. About this date, or a little earlier, the baudrick was introduced.[2] At first it appears on civilians, and from it the dagger was slung on the right side, which was also adopted from the anelace of civil dress, for every franklin carried his

[1] The effigy of Sir John Lyons, Warkworth, Northamptonshire, living 1346, is usually given as the latest example of the cyclas.

[2] The effigy of the youth William of Hatfield, who died in 1335, is represented in his effigy at York wearing a baudrick over a delicately embroidered tight-fitting cote-hardie, and fastened by a large stud on the left side. In front is a loop for the anelace. This is an early civil example of the baudrick.

PLATE XI.

Fig. 24.

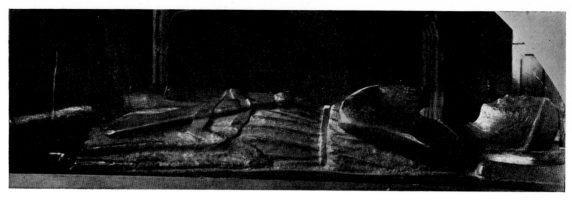

SIR PHILIP GAYTON (DIED 1316). GAYTON, NORTHANTS.

Fig. 25.

? SIR WALTER TREYLLI AND DAME ELEANOR TREYLLI (DIED 1316). WOODFORD, NORTHANTS.

Fig. 26.

? JOAN, 1ST WIFE OF SIR ROBERT ACHARD (*c.* 1320). SPARSHOLT, BERKS.

To face page 45.

dagger at his girdle. "In woodcraft the baudrick was the special band for suspending the hunting-horn from the neck, and the points or 'tyndes' of a hart's horn were reckoned in the Middle Ages so soon as a baudrick, or a lyam or leash, could be hung to them."[1]

The series of wooden effigies includes as many as five knights in the jupon, a garment composed of several thicknesses of material sewed through and faced with silk or velvet, upon which were embroidered the wearer's arms. At Sparsholt, Berkshire, we find a knight and two ladies, which are supposed to represent Sir Robert Achard and his two wives. The first wife, Joan, died in 1336. The knight rests his head upon his tilting helmet with its mutilated crest, while his head is encased in the bascinet with the camail attached to it; beneath the jupon can be seen his shirt of mail. This effigy must be an early instance of the jupon as a military garment.

At Millom in Cumberland, and at Southacre in Norfolk, are mutilated fragments of wooden effigies of knights. The first is that of some member of the Huddlestone family, whose ancient stronghold is near the church. The second is probably of Sir Alexander Harsick, and not, as Gough says, of "the first of that surname." Fortunately the Rev. T. Kerrich made a drawing of this effigy[2] in 1779, when it was in a less mutilated condition, and from this drawing we are able to see that the knight was portrayed as wearing a jupon and a baudrick. He has no bascinet or camail, for his head is uncovered and the hair is worn long.

The cracked and sadly mutilated effigy of a knight at Heveningham, Suffolk, has been attributed to Sir John Heveningham, who died in 1452, or the following year; but as the figure

---

[1] See *Sword Belts of the Middle Ages*, by Albert Hartshorne, and *Archæological Journal*, XLVIII, 334.

[2] Kerrich MS. Coll. (British Museum) 6,730, p. 61.

is represented in a jupon it must therefore belong to some earlier knight, as this military garment [went out of fashion by 1413, some forty years before Sir John Heveningham's effigy could have been made.

In the recess in the south wall of the sanctuary of Tickencote Church, Rutland, is an effigy to a knight which has also suffered from decay and neglect. The head is protected by a bascinet, to which is attached a camail; the jupon is adorned with fringe of fleurs-de-lys, and the baudrick has been richly ornamented. It is surmised that this effigy was to Sir Roland le Dameys. He was knighted in 1355 and was living in 1388.

At Cold Higham, Northamptonshire, is a wooden effigy which is a most instructive example of the transitional period of armour. It represents Sir John Pateshull, who died in 1350. The cyclas had then gone out of fashion and the jupon had been adopted in its place; yet Sir John Pateshull is depicted in a surcoat with mail hauberk and hose of the early part of the fourteenth century; while the bascinet, camail, circular elbow-cops with single articulation, leather gauntlets having articulated fingers and articulated knee-cops, are indicative of the middle part of the century. The head rests on two low cushions, the lower one rectangular and the upper one lozenge-shaped, such as occur in the earlier period; while at the feet is a lion, less fierce than many we find as the century advances.

The wooden effigy of a knight at Chew Magna, Somerset, is said to have been brought from Norton Church, which was destroyed at the time of the Reformation. It represents a knight in transitional armour of about the middle of the fourteenth century. The knight reclines on his left side, resting on his hip and left elbow. Between the left elbow and the hip lies the shield. The right arm is brought over the breast and the hand rests on the edge of the shield. The left leg is raised from the hip and the foot placed against the side of a lion, whose open mouth is turned towards the effigy. The artist has represented this knight in prick spurs and a surcoat. This military garment was being abandoned at the time this effigy was carved; the fashion of wearing the cyclas had nearly run its course; and the jupon was being adopted by a few military men. The defences for the arms and legs, now painted to represent plate armour, were intended, probably, to depict chain-mail with plate or cuir-bouilli reinforcements. No mail is now indicated in colour, but this would not have been the case when the figure was originally decorated. The hands are in leather gauntlets with gadlings, and the feet appear to be encased in flexible leather coverings like gloves, showing the outline of the toes,[1] while the defence for the head is a round-topped helmet having a small visor attached on pivots, which could be lowered to protect the eyes and nose. Beneath this helmet was, possibly, a semi-globular bascinet to which was attached a camail, and over the latter falls from under the helmet an unusual adjunct which has now a rigid appearance like metal plates, but may have been intended merely for mantling. This figure was probably carved between 1340 and 1350. Tradition has long assigned this effigy to Sir John Hauteville, who lived in the reign of Henry III. The last Hauteville, however, was Geoffrey, who parted with the manor of Norton in 1328 to John Wych, and on his death, in 1346, his wife Egelina married Robert Cheyne of Lincolnshire, and through her he became possessed of the manor and advowson of the church of Norton. The date 1346 agrees so well with the period when this effigy was carved that it is probable it

---

[1] The feet of the wooden effigy of a knight at Whorlton, Yorkshire, appear as if they were uncovered, and the toes are more visible than is the case of the Chew Magna knight. The late Sir William Hope conjectured that they were encased in flexible leather like gloves, as the spurs could hardly have been attached to bare ankles.

represents John Wych who died in that year, and neither a Hauteville nor a member of the Cheyne family.

Effigies of knights in romantic attitudes were carved during the first half of the fourteenth century at various centres,[1] and at Aldworth,[2] Berkshire, we find a stone knight very similar to the wooden figure at Chew Magna in a natural and dramatic attitude. The manner of disposal of the legs of both knights is nearly identical;[3] the defences for the head and neck are unusual but not dissimilar; the reinforcements of plate or cuir-bouilli form a strong resemblance, although details vary; while at a time when the camail was in use each knight is clothed in a flowing surcoat, open in front showing the hauberk, and falling between the legs in folds under the left knee.

The Aldworth knight is made from a yellow stone conveyed from East Gloucestershire by way of the Thames to Abingdon, where it was, probably, carved.[4] The authors of *Medieval Figure-Sculpture in England* [5] consider that the gifted craftsman who made this effigy appears to have "almost modelled a

[1] Romantic figures were made in the Exeter workshops during the first half of the fourteenth century; others may be seen at Burgh Green, Cambridgeshire, and Reepham and Ingham, Norfolk, and in other parts of England. See illustrations by Stothard, and *Archæological Journal*, XXXIV, 502.

[2] See Effigy in Aldworth Church, Berkshire, and some notice of the de la Beche family of that county, *Archæological Journal*, XXXIV, 502.

[3] The arms of the Aldworth effigy are lost, yet it is probable they were disposed like the Chew Magna knight.

[4] Prior and Gardner's *Medieval Figure-Sculpture in England*, Fig. 727, p. 649.

[5] Alexander of Abingdon was one of the craftsmen employed on the figure-sculpture of the "Eleanor" crosses (*c.* 1292). We know he had a workshop in London and was a London citizen, yet, for all that he may have had a close connection with the atelier at Abingdon where the Aldworth effigies were executed. Prof. Prior and Mr. A. Gardner compare his work on the Waltham "Eleanor" with a "Lady" in Aldworth Church (*c.* 1300), and find a strong resemblance between them. It is possible that this remarkable sculptor exercised an influence over work turned out from the Abingdon workshop. See Lethaby's *Westminster Abbey, the King's Craftsman*, 177, 245; and Prior and Gardner's *Medieval Figure-Sculpture in England*, 349.

PLATE XII.

PLATE XII.

Fig. 27,

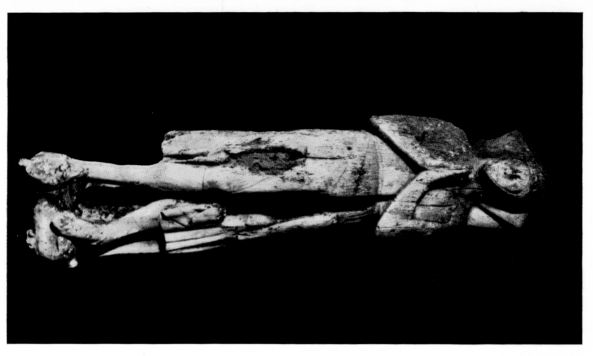

SIR WILLIAM COMBMARTIN (*c.* 1320).   ALDERTON, NORTHANTS.

Fig. 28,

KNIGHT OF THE REYNES FAMILY, AND WIFE (*c.* 1330).   CLIFTON REYNES, BUCKS.

' dying Gaul ' in the type of Pergamene sculpture." It is probable that the Aldworth knight is some twenty years earlier than the Chew Magna figure, yet it is quite possible that the same imager may have carved both. In any case it seems nearly certain that the Chew Magna effigy emanated from the Abingdon school of art, and the brilliant idealism of the medieval sculptor can still be discerned in the cruelly mutilated stone knight at Aldworth and the over-restored wooden effigy at Chew Magna.[1]

There appear to be no wooden effigies after the middle of the fourteenth century until we meet with those at Wingfield, which were made about 1415. It seems as if the frightful devastation caused by the Black Death had killed off most of the imagers and carvers in wood, as we find no wooden effigies during the period of the most serious ravages of this terrible epidemic.

The beautiful monument of Michael de la Pole, second Earl of Suffolk, and his countess, who was the daughter of Hugh Earl of Stafford, is in Wingfield Church, Suffolk. The earl, who is described as a knight of " the most excellent and knightly reputation," accompanied King Henry V on his military expedition into France, and died of dysentery in 1415 while the English were besieging Harfleur. The countess was one of his executors, and it is probable that she erected this fine monument to her husband and herself soon after his death. The earl is depicted in the transitional period of armour, and he wears a jupon, and a gorget of plate over the camail. " The great simplicity of this plain suit of plate armour which he wears," wrote Mr. Stothard, " personifies the idea which we entertain of the appearance of the martial spectre so boldly imagined by Shakespeare for one of his finest dramas." The effigy of the countess is very beautiful, and the elegant folds

[1] See *Proc. Som. Arch. Soc.*, LXVII, 22–5.

D

of the drapery are not far removed from similar work of an earlier date. The countess is dressed in kirtle, super-tunic, and long mantle with a deep collar, and the folds caught up over the arms. A broad belt with a large buckle encircles the waist ; while the head-dress has a fret with a beautiful pattern of four-leaved flowers set in squares. A golden circlet encloses her veil, which falls to her neck. The tomb is remarkable in so far that the side facing the chancel serves as the sedilia for the high altar ; while the constant recurrence of the Stafford knot indicates the badge of the countess's family. Both effigies are sculptured with great care, and are valuable examples of armour and costume of the time of Henry V. The artist gives evidence of great capacity for taking infinite pains with his work ; and if this monument does not quite express the high artistic genius of the early years of the previous century, yet it is a fine work of art, and we deplore the fact that it is only a hundred years since a thick coating of paint was spread over these figures hiding the resplendent gilding and colouring which adorned the gesso work. Wooden monumental effigies were not frequently made after the middle of the fourteenth century, and these memorials to an Earl and Countess of Suffolk (c. 1415) are rare examples of fifteenth-century craftsmanship in oak. They appear to possess no affinity in style with those alabaster figures which were being made at Chellaston in Derbyshire and to be more akin with those that emanated from London workshops. Sir William Hope's suggestion that they may possibly have been wooden patterns for alabaster carvings is not altogether an unlikely one.[1]

The mid-point of architecture as Gothic expression was reached 1270–1290, and was on the decline before wooden

[1] The alabaster effigy of Margaret Holland with her two husbands in Canterbury Cathedral (Prior and Gardner's *Medieval Figure-Sculpture in England*, 700, Fig. 790), although of a later date, bear comparison in head-dress and drapery with the Countess of Suffolk at Wingfield in detail and technique.

effigies appear to have been extensively made. The examples
we possess dating from the closing years of the thirteenth century and the early years of the fourteenth century show that
the wooden effigy then reached a high standard of excellence
both in carving and surface decoration. When Gothic architecture fell from its high estate they, too, declined in beauty
and refinement. After 1350 the stone figures lost much of
their style, and the wooden figures seem to have passed
away for a time altogether.

The series of wooden effigies includes twelve ladies whose
dates vary from about 1290 to 1350, and their costume during
these sixty years shows very little variation in fashion. The
dress is most simple, consisting of a kirtle with long buttoned
sleeves and over it a sleeveless cote-hardie with a long flowing
mantle fastened over the breast by cords passing through fer-
mailes. A wimple is usually worn round the neck hiding the
chin and sides of the face, while the hair is kept in place by a
narrow encircled fillet, and sometimes a single plait or curl
appears on either side of the forehead. On the head is a veil
or coverchief, falling in elegant folds to the shoulders.

Two of the wooden effigies to ladies were most probably
sculptured before the close of the thirteenth century. The one
to Margaret, second wife of Adam of Everingham, at Laxton,
Nottinghamshire, has already been described. She survived her
husband, who died in 1287. The other is to a lady at Little
Horkesley, Essex, and she was possibly the wife of Sir William
Horkesley, who died in 1296. The costume of these two Nottinghamshire and Essex ladies is very similar save that the
Horkesley lady has a shorter mantle. These two effigies and
the one to Dame Eleanor Treylli, at Woodford, Northamptonshire, who died in 1316, are typical examples of the series we
are now considering. The two ladies at Clifton Reynes,
Buckinghamshire, are in the costumes of this period: the one

dates from about 1310, and was the wife of Sir Ralph Reynes, and the other about fifteen years later. At Dodford, North-amptonshire, is an effigy in wood which probably represents Hawise Keynes, a melancholy wreck of a once beautiful figure; while at Hildersham, Cambridgeshire, is the wooden figure of a lady which was long believed to represent the wife of Sir Thomas Busteler. He died, however, in 1370, and the effigies attributed to him and his wife must belong to a much earlier date.

In the south wall of the church at Little Baddow, Essex, are two niches forming a double canopied high tomb. The fronts consist of panels containing a series of quatrefoils in circles within each of which is an uncharged heater-shaped shield. The canopies are flat ogee arches slightly tilted, and each arch has fine cuspings, while between the arches and the crocketings are spandrels. Moulded jambs support the arches, which run up to the string course, terminating in square bosses. Grouped with the monument is a piscina possessing a canopy and crocketing of the same date and character. The effigies are protected by wrought-iron scrolled stanchions, very dilapidated, and half of them are missing. The lady wears a kirtle with tight-fitting sleeves fastened with twenty-four buttons, cote-hardie, wimple and veil, reposing on one tomb, while her husband rests on the other. These figures probably represent members of the Filliol family, who at that time possessed the manor of Little Baddow.

There is a beautiful effigy of a lady at Englefield, Berkshire, which is illustrated by T. and G. Hollis in their *Monumental Effigies of Great Britain*. She is dressed in a long gown worn high in the neck, with tight-fitting sleeves. The mantle falls to within 1 foot 6 inches of the bottom of the kirtle, and is gathered in plaits at the neck. Over it is a collar, 2½ inches deep, and folded back under the head; and a wimple is worn

PLATE XIII.

Fig. 29.

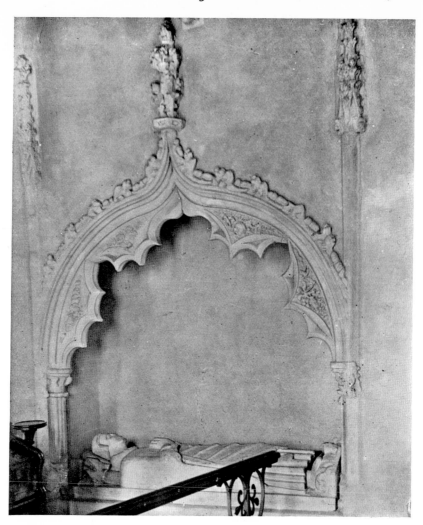

? VICAR (*c.* 1320).   LITTLE LEIGHS, ESSEX.

Fig. 30.

? HAWISE KEYNES (*c.* 1330).   DODFORD, NORTHANTS.

To face page 53.

round the chin and fastened under a linen coif. Of the original colouring there are now no remains. The two ladies at Sparsholt, Berkshire, both wear wimples and veils; and the mutilated effigy at Barkham, in the same county, is in a similar dress, and is supposed to represent Anne, daughter and heiress of Thomas Neville. She married Gilbert Bullock, who was living in 1336. The effigy of the wife of Sir Lawrence Pavely, at Paulespury, Northamptonshire, is a work of high artistic quality, and the gathered-up folds of the drapery have been well executed. This effigy probably dates about 1350. A little earlier in date, but very similar in costume, is a wooden effigy at Tawstock in Devon. It is supposed to represent Thomasin, daughter of Sir Richard Hankford, and wife of Sir William Bourchier, created Lord Fitz Warine in 1448–9, but this is quite impossible. The effigy shows the lady as wearing a wimple and coverchief edged with lace, and her mantle is caught up over the arms, descending in graceful folds, while it is fastened by two bands secured on each side by jewelled buckles or studs. This effigy, with the head resting on a large rectangular cushion and the mantle brought across the body, being a Bristol mannerism, was carved in the capital of the West of England (1330–1340), and having been shipped to Barnstaple was taken on the River Taw to its destination.

The effigies of Ralph Neville, second Earl of Westmorland, and his second wife Margaret, daughter of Reginald, Lord Cobham, rest on a wooden tomb in the middle of the chancel of Brancepeth Church, county Durham. Leland speaks of this monument as a "high tombe," but since his day it has been cut down, and now the entablature only rests on the base and plinth. The earl is in armour, and beneath the tabard escalloped at the bottom is the skirt of mail. The legs are encased in cuisses, articulated knee-cops, and jambs, and the feet in articulated sollerets. The hands are depicted in cuffed gauntlets, the sword is slung on the left side by a transverse belt, and the baudrick is meagre, although richly ornamented. Over the armour is worn a collar of suns and roses,[1] and the pendant is the white boar of Richard III. The head-piece is a visored salade with its chin-piece. In action the visor was brought down over the face so as to join the gorget. In this effigy, however, no artifice could ever bring the eye-slits in useful proximity to the earl's eyes, and the chin-piece seems equally shorn of its true proportion. However, we can respect the motive of the artist whose device was to bring into view the earl's countenance. This particular head defence is rarely seen on monumental effigies. There is one in Meriden Church, Warwickshire,[2] and Viscount Dillon also points out an instance of one on a beautiful effigy of a Martin in Piddletown Church, Dorset.[3] In brasses it is met with in that of Robert Staunton (1458) at Castle Donington, Leicestershire,[4] and in that of Edmund Clere (1488) in Stokesley Church, Norfolk.[5] Abroad the salade and its chin-piece are fairly frequent in Germany.[6] The earl died in 1484, and some writers have considered that his armour belongs to an earlier date. One authority has even gone so far as to compare it with that worn by Edward, Prince of Wales, who died in 1376. It may be that the absence of tuilles gives the armour the appearance of being antiquated and out of date. The gorget, however, resembles those on the

[1] Collars of this kind belong to the period of 1461–1485.

[2] This effigy is figured in Bloxam's *Monumental Architecture.*

[3] See *Archæological Journal*, LV, 119. This effigy dates from 1471–5.

[4] Boutell's *Series of Monumental Brasses.*

[5] Cotman's *Brasses of Norfolk*, I, Plate 36.

[6] Viscount Dillon gives a list of several on the Continent (*Archæological Journal*, LV, 119) : Henneberg effigy (1490) ; Albrecht Dürer's " Death and the Knight " and his portraits of the Brothers Baumgartner (1506) ; bas-relief on the Porto Nuovo at Naples of Alphonso the Victorious and his companions which was executed in 1470 ; and in the Uffizi Gallery at Florence is a portrait of Erasmo da Narni (Gattamelata) and his squire by Giorgione (1438–41). The squire wears the chin-piece, but instead of the salade he is seen in the cap only.

Wimborne and Tong knights, and the visored salade, as we have already noted, is found on effigies of this period. The upper portion of the armour might have the date 1475 assigned to it, and the lower part might belong to about 1430. The countess wears a kirtle made very low in front with tight-fitting mitten sleeves, a sideless cote-hardie with deep facings most likely of fur ; a girdle worn loosely is attached to an ornament of suns similar to those of the collar, and the long mantle is fastened by cords attached to ornamental studs. Round the neck is a collar of roses *en soleil*, and the pendant has a lozenge-shaped jewel set in gold. The head-dress is a shortened form of the steeple, and the veil has been held on the cushion by three figures now destroyed. The head-dress shows the transition between the steeple and the pedimental coiffure. At the feet have been two small figures (destroyed) of clerks kneeling at desks on which are laid open books resembling the diminutive couple at the feet of the stone effigy of Archbishop Chichele (*c.* 1440) at Canterbury,[1] and the four kneeling Vicar's choral at the feet of an alabaster dignitary (*c.* 1450) in the chapel of St. Calixtus, Wells Cathedral.[2] These effigies were probably made in London, and Sir William Hope suggested that these wooden effigies, like those at Wingfield, Suffolk, were merely patterns mentioned in contracts for the monuments, and not the finished effigies which would have been of alabaster.

[1] Prior and Gardner's *Medieval Figure-Sculpture in England*, 713, Fig. 811.
[2] *Proc. Som. Arch. Soc.*, LXIX, Plate V. Another instance is on the stone " Ecclesiastic " at St. Bartholomew's, Smithfield.

PLATE XIV.

Fig. 31.

KNIGHT (*c.* 1330).   BURES, SUFFOLK.

Fig. 32.

? AGNES, 2ND WIFE OF SIR ROBERT ACHARD (*c.* 1340).   SPARSHOLT, BERKS.

PART III

REVIVAL OF WOODEN EFFIGIES IN THE SIXTEENTH AND SEVENTEENTH CENTURIES

WOODEN monumental effigies went out of fashion soon after the middle of the fourteenth century, but were again revived in the sixteenth, and the first on our list is the one to Edmund Cornewall, at Burford, Shropshire, son and heir of Sir Thomas Cornewall, who died in 1508 in his twentieth year. This fine effigy rests on a wooden chest decorated with eight shields of arms, and is clad in a complete suit of plate armour of the Tudor period. The skirt of mail is scarcely visible on the effigy of this young man, but on some brasses and effigies of this date it appears below the taces and even reaches beyond the tuilles. The feet are in sabbatons, or broad-toed shoes, and rest against a crowned dog, while two angels reposing on the helmet support the uncovered head with their hands. The hair is worn long and falls to the neck covering the ears; the face is clean-shaven, but not so youthful in appearance as we might expect under the circumstances; there is neither sword nor spurs.

Fourteen years later (1522) was made the remarkable wooden tomb and effigy of Sir Roger Rockley, at Worsborough, Yorkshire. This monument, or hearse, consists of a chest adorned with shields of arms of the Rochley and Mountency families, with another tier and canopy above. The canopy

57

projects, and is adorned with trefoils and circles united with a running scroll. On the chest is the ghastly cadaver in an open shroud, and above rests the squire in plate armour with a helmet on his head with the visor raised. The hair is worn long, the face clean-shaven, while the countenance shows a youthful expression; yet the knight could not have been very young, as he had married twice, and his son and heir was six years old at the time of his death.

We have already referred to wooden tombs bearing wooden effigies of William of Valence in Westminster Abbey, at Worsborough in Yorkshire, Pitchford and Burford in Shropshire, Brancepeth and Staindrop in county Durham, and the fragment at All Saints' Church, Derby, which has been so skilfully inserted in the modern restoration. Conspicuous among this class is the remarkable one at Thornhill, Yorkshire, sustaining the figures of Sir John Saville and his two wives, Alice Vernon and Elizabeth Paston. The tomb is adorned with carving and shields of arms, and when originally constructed it must have presented the appearance of a four-post bed with the curious arrangement of a knight placed between his two wives. On the edge of the tomb is the following inscription: *Bonys emong stonys lys here ful styl qwylste the sawle wanderis were that God wyl in Anno DM mill (es) imo quingentissimo vigesimo nono.* The knight is in a suit of plate armour; his hair is worn long falling to his neck; and his face exhibits such sharp characteristic features that we venture to conjecture that it is intended for a portrait of Sir John Saville. The ladies are dressed in kirtles with tight-fitting sleeves, having bands at the wrists and an ornamental border at the neck. The long mantles are fastened across the breast with a decorated band having gold studs. Their wavy hair is worn long, falling to the elbows, while their veils are enclosed in golden fillets adorned with deeply cut Tudor roses bound round their temples.

PLATE XV.

Fig. 33.

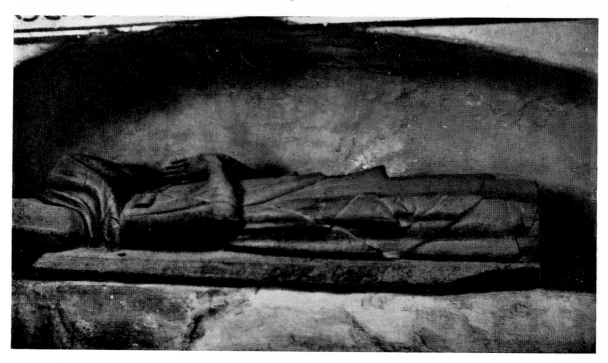

LADY (1330–40). TAWSTOCK, DEVON.

Fig. 34.

KNIGHT OF THE POLLARD FAMILY (*c.* 1340). AUCKLAND, CO. DURHAM.

To face page 59.

Such a memorial as we have been considering is usually dated by the middle figure, who, probably, gave the order during life for the common monument, or left instructions to the executors to carry out its erection. The execution, technique and the precise parallelism of the ladies in similar costume on either side of the knight, whose straight legs and hands folded on the breast form an exact centre line, indicate the cut-and-dried product of the workshop.

Eight years after this striking monument had been placed in Thornhill Church, the effigies of Sir Alexander Culpeper and his wife Constance Agnes were executed for the church of St. Mary the Virgin, at Goudhurst, Kent. The knight is exhibited in a fine suit of engraved plate armour; his head is bare and rests on a helmet adorned with oak leaves, and placed on a large square cushion having corner tassels; while the neck is encircled by a heavy gold chain, but the pendant is hidden by the knight's folded hands. Over his cuirass is a tabard, a most important ornament of knightly equipment. In modern times this has been painted white and flowered with a red pattern; but it is more probable that originally this heraldic coat, reaching below the skirt of the taces, would be charged with the wearer's armorial bearings. It has short sleeves on which the arms would also be repeated.[1] The lady is dressed in petticoat, waistcoat with attached sleeves, and gown having long open sleeves lined with fur and fastened across the breast with a band attached to two golden ornaments. The feet are encased in broad-toed shoes, the girdle has golden tassels, and round her neck are as many as five gold chains, and also a necklace with gold pendant. Her pedimental head-dress was probably made of black velvet or silk, the top stiffened to the shape of a

---

[1] The tabard occasionally appears in the Yorkist period, but did not come into anything like general use until the reigns of Henry VII and Henry VIII. It is rarely found later than the sixteenth century.

sloping roof, the edges falling on either side, made stiff so as to stand parallel, and these may have been sewn with gold or pearls. The ends of the hood would hang down the back, but cannot be seen. This is surmounted by a stiffened material also richly adorned with jewels, and the whole pinned on to a close-fitting cap of a different colour, the edges of which show above the forehead. At the bottom of the head-dress on the left side hangs a gold ornament with a Cupid upon it. On the east wall, above the tomb, is a small bas-relief bearing the date 1537. The knight and the lady are depicted as kneeling at a prayer-desk with their children behind them, while above is represented St. George slaying the dragon, the Blessed Virgin with the Holy Child, and our Saviour in the clouds.

In the church of St. Mary the Virgin at Slyndon, Sussex, is the effigy of a knight which is assigned to Sir Anthony St. Ledger (locally "Sellinger"), whose will, dated 1539, directs his burial to be in Slyndon Church. The armour is plate, and a good example of that worn in the middle of the Tudor period. The vambraces are fluted, the tuilles are channelled, the elbow and knee-cops show Renaissance work, the head is uncovered, the hair long and clubbed, the head rests on a tilting helmet, and the feet are encased in broad-toed sabbatons adorned with Renaissance scrolling. The knight has neither spurs nor sword.

The beautiful wooden monument at Worsborough, Yorkshire, gives some faint conception of what the splendid tomb to the memory of three of the family of Games of Aberbrân and their three wives must have presented when it was first erected in the chancel of the priory church of St. John the Evangelist at Brecon, now the Cathedral Church of the diocese of Swansea and Brecon.

At Worsborough there are only two tiers, with one figure on each bed, but at Brecon there were " three tiers of oaken beds," with two effigies on each bed. This tomb must therefore have been truly magnificent in its carving, gilding, and colour, rising to a height of at least 10 or 12 feet.

Churchyard visited Brecon in 1587, and in his rhyming description says that on this monument

> Three couple lies one ore the other's head
> Along in tombe and all one race and lyne.
>
> *   *   *   *   *
>
> These are indeede the auncient race of Gams
> A house and blood that long rich armes doth give
> And now in Wales are many of their names
> That keepe great trayne and doth full bravely live.

Fifty-eight years (1645) after Churchyard had written these lines, Richard Symonds, a captain in King Charles the First's army, visited Brecon, and mentioned this tomb in his Diary,[1] and about forty years later Thomas Dineley gives a sad description of the complete destruction of five of the effigies. He records that in the chancel "is seen a Wooden Monument wth as wooden Rimes about it in old English Character, there is but one large figure left thereon the rest was sayd to be burned by ye Usurpers souldiers, it belonged to a good Family of Game's of Aberbrain."[2]

It was not until the early part of the nineteenth century that the monument was removed, and it is a lasting disgrace that a Fellow of the Society of Antiquaries should say: "Only one female figure remained when this vile incumbrance was removed; the rest . . . were burnt by the commonwealth soldiers; much as I deplore the outrages they committed, I have often lamented, while it continued, that they did not destroy the whole of it. Lord Camden has, however, with great

---

[1] Diary of *Richard Symonds*, published by the Camden Society in 1859. Original MS. 17062 British Museum. He mentions that the armorial bearings on the tomb were " a chevron between 3 spears' heads, crest, a wreath, a wyvern, gules." These were the arms of the family of Games of Aberbrân.

[2] *The Progress of the Duke of Beaufort through Wales in 1684*, by Thomas Dineley. Copied from the original MS. at Badminton (London, 1888), 210.

propriety, lately caused it to be taken down, and the chancel decently and uniformly painted."[1]

The one figure remaining is the effigy of a lady of about the year 1555, dressed in gown, tight sleeves, petticoat, and elaborately plaited super tunic, tied round the waist with a scarf. A French hood, single ruffs round the neck and the wrists, and a pomander is hung from the waist by a long chain. This is the age of heavy chains, and two adorn the neck of the lady. Her arms and face are mutilated, and her effigy is the only fragment remaining of a splendid wooden monument which once occupied a prominent position in one of the most stately churches in the principality of Wales.

Queen Elizabeth had been reigning two years (1560) when the splendid wooden monument was erected at Staindrop, county Durham, to Henry Neville, fifth Earl of Westmorland, and his two wives.[2] The east end of the tomb was divided into three compartments filled with heraldic shields, the west end was similar, but is now destroyed. The two sides contain kneeling figures of the eight sons and daughters of the earl, and are valuable examples of the costume of children in the reign of Queen Bess. One boy is in tunic and hose, and the others in long gowns with wide collars, single ruffs, and hair worn long. The girls are all dressed in gowns open at the neck, loose girdles tied in knots in front, super-tunics with wide hanging sleeves, and French caps. The earl is exhibited in a suit of armour of the early years of Queen Elizabeth. The cuirass is long-waisted, the pauldrons are replaced by shoulder-

[1] Theophilus Jones, *History of the County of Brecknock* (Brecknock, 1809), II, Part i, 41.

[2] The earl married three times ; and these effigies represent Jane and Margaret, being his second and third wives. They were the daughters of Sir Roger Cholmeley, and the first lady was the widow of Sir Henry Gascoigne. Queen Elizabeth was furious at the earl marrying his deceased wife's sister, and he was tried before the Bishop of Durham and the Archbishop of York, as Metropolitan, in the Ecclesiastical Court, but he died before the case was concluded.

PLATE XVI.

Fig. 35.

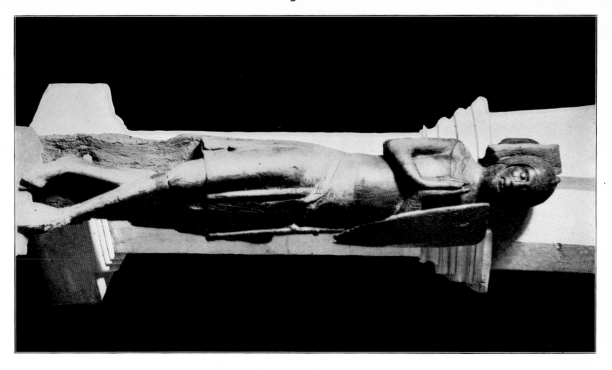

SIR THOMAS LE LATIMER (DIED 1334).   BRAYBROOKE, NORTHANTS.

Fig. 36.

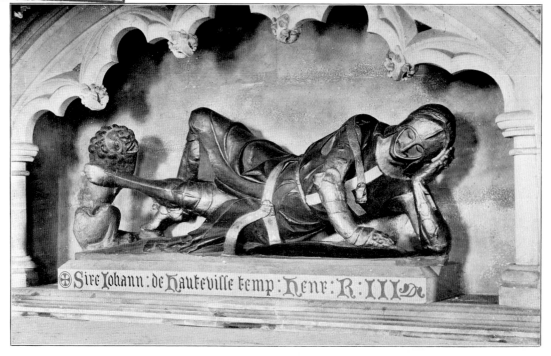

? JOHN WYCH (DIED 1346).   CHEW MAGNA, SOMERSET.

pieces, the skirt of taces has not yet disappeared, and they end in a series of narrow fluted and pointed pendent plates 2½ inches long. Beneath these plates can be seen the skirt of mail. The knee-cops and elbow-cops are adorned with human faces having their tongues exposed. The gorget is decorated with Tudor roses, and round the neck is a gold chain with a George. The head is bare, resting on a crest, a bull's head; the hair is now worn short, the moustaches are drooping, and the beard is divided into two points. The ladies are dressed in gowns plaited from the waist, and V-shaped in front so as to show the petticoat beneath with its decorated border. The sleeves are highly ornamental, and were doubtless attached to the gown, and both ladies wear French caps adorned with Tudor roses, gold chains with pendants encircle their necks, and small ruffs are round their necks and wrists.[1]

On a brick tomb at Boxted, Suffolk, protected by spiked railings, repose the effigies of William Poley and his wife, Alice Shaa. The lady died in 1579 and her husband eight years later (1587). He is exhibited in plate armour, and buckled immediately to his cuirass are tassets, the legitimate development of the tuilles, but consisting of several plates. These hang over the trunk breeches, which are embroidered. The sollerets are round-toed, the sword-belt is ornamented, the uncovered head rests on a tilting helmet, the curly hair is worn short, the beard is pointed in the form known as the *pique davant* style, the moustaches are particularly long and drooping, and the unknightly appendages of ruffs encircle the neck and wrists. The lady wears a gown high in the neck and divided

---

[1] Compare this wooden memorial with the alabaster one in the same church to Ralph Neville, 1st Earl of Westmorland (died 1425), and two of his three wives, with the monument and effigies in Canterbury Cathedral to Margaret Holland and her two husbands (*c.* 1440), and with the wooden tomb and effigies to Sir John Saville (died 1529) and his two wives, Thornhill, Yorkshire. These symmetrically placed figures denote the product of workshop sculpture.

in front to show the petticoat. Ruffs are worn round the neck and wrists, and from the girdle is suspended a prayer book, the back of which is carved with a lozenge containing the Poley impaling the Shaa arms. The head is in a jewelled French cap, and as this was the age of gold chains, we find three encircling the neck, and narrow chain bracelets are also worn round the wrists.

It is conjectured that the effigy at Thruxton, Hampshire, is to Lady Elizabeth Phillpotts. She wears a tight-fitting French cap made of linen with a horseshoe-shaped front, and a short lappet or veil hanging down behind. The outer gown is straight, without waistband or girdle, and is open in front showing the petticoat. It is, however, long-waisted, and has a straight and formal stomacher with an invected edging. The sleeves are tight, and a farthingale puffs out the petticoat over the hips; the bodice is square at the neck and there is a ruff. The hands are broken, and there were doubtless also ruffs at the wrists.

We now approach the closing years of the sixteenth century, and in the chancel of St. Giles' Church, Durham, we find the wooden figure of John Heath of Kepier, who died in 1590. This effigy is truly wooden in every sense of the word. We know not what it looked like before it suffered restoration in 1843, but now we are at once reminded of Don Quixote when we behold it. The figure is represented in plate armour; at the bottom of the cuirass is an escalloped edging of three borders, round the neck is a gorget of plate, a collar with narrow slits in it and a ruff, the head is uncovered and rests on a tilting helmet surmounted by a crest of a cock's head attached to a wreath, the twisted hilt of the sword has a round pommel and is suspended by a strap over the right shoulder, the feet are in sollerets and rest against a scroll enfolding two death's heads. On the upper part of this scroll are the words HODIE MICHI, and in the lower part CRAS TIBI.

PLATE XVII.

Fig. 37.

LADY OF ENGLEFIELD FAMILY (*c.* 1340). ENGLEFIELD, BERKS.

Fig. 38.

? SIR THOMAS CRESACRE (*c.* 1345). BARNBOROUGH, YORKS.

Fig. 39.

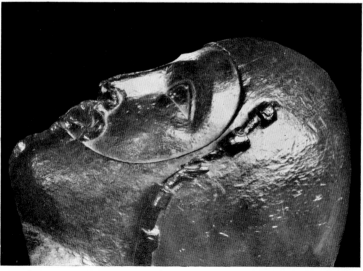

? SIR THOMAS CRESACRE (*c.* 1345). BARNBOROUGH, YORKS.

To face page 65.

In the earlier part of this volume (page 30) we have already referred to the seventeenth-century wooden effigy of the Rev. Joseph Collier, rector of Steeple Langford, Wiltshire (1607–1635), when describing the ecclesiastical effigies still existing in England.[1]

In the Oglander chapel in St. Mary's Church, Brading, Isle of Wight, are three wooden effigies. The one on the south side is that of Sir William Oglander, knight, who died in 1608. From the will of his son, Sir John Oglander, dated 10th November, 1640, we find that this effigy was at that date at Nunewell. It is a fine work of art, and was carved at Newport for the sum of £33. It is fully coloured, and represents Sir William Oglander in plate armour of the period of James I. On the north side of the chapel is the effigy of his son, Sir John Oglander, knight, the author of the famous Oglander Manuscript Memoirs. He is represented in plate armour of an earlier period with a shield and helmet of a later date. He lies on his right side, with crossed legs and resting his head on his right hand, suggesting a comparison with the attitude of the wooden effigy probably of John Wych, now in Chew Magna Church, Somerset. It has been conjectured that possibly Sir John restored for his own use some earlier effigy and added to it a shield and helmet of a later date. However, it possesses little merit in execution; the legs are clumsy and the right arm is sadly out of proportion. In 1640 this effigy was already prepared, and Sir John mentions it in his will, stating that it is in the Oglander Chapel. There is no doubt that Sir John was so highly pleased with this figure that he left instructions to his executor to prepare a diminutive reproduction for his only son George, who died of smallpox contracted at Caen in Normandy during a tour he took after his coming of age. This small effigy is only 1 foot 9 inches long, and is placed

---

[1] No ecclesiastical wooden effigies are now existing in Wales.

E

in a recess above the tomb of his father in the north wall of the Oglander chapel. It is similar in every detail to the large figure on the altar tomb beneath it, with the exception that the face is that of a young man without moustaches, that the feet are not armed with spurs, and that the sword is bent near the point.

Whether wooden effigies were largely employed in other countries we do not know. That erudite scholar, the late Hefner von Alteneck, in a letter to Mr. Albert Hartshorne, remarks that there is not one now existing in Germany. This statement must be received with some degree of reserve, as there is a wooden effigy to an ecclesiastic at Hildesheim, and there are possibly others. It is probable that there are also some in Italy. In Burgos Cathedral Church in Spain there is a wooden effigy of an English ecclesiastic, and it is possible that it was made in England and sent out to that country. In Ireland there may be a few. There is a wooden figure of an ecclesiastic in Eucharistic vestments within a small church styled Teach Molaise, on Tory Island, county Donegal, which tradition ascribed to St. Molaise, and is said to be the work of the celebrated Goban Saor. Whether this has been a monumental effigy or the figurehead of some ill-fated ship of the Spanish Armada it is difficult to say.[1] However, it seems probable that our English effigies in wood are some of the finest existing in Europe, and we are thankful that the ravages of time and the relentless hand of the modern restorer have still left us some treasures which we may consider representative of a great national school of medieval handicraft. The earliest record of a wooden effigy in England is the one to Cadwgan, Bishop of Bangor,[2] who died as a monk at Abbey Dore in Herefordshire

---

[1] See *Programme of Excursion*, June 21–29, 1904, *Royal Society of Antiquaries of Ireland*, p. 14.

[2] Gough, II, civ.

PLATE XVIII.

Fig. 40.

SIR JOHN PATESHULL (DIED 1349). COLD HIGHAM, NORTHANTS.

Fig. 41.

SIR LAURENCE PAVELY (DIED 1349). PAULESPURY, NORTHANTS.

Fig. 42.

DAME PAVELY (*c.* 1350). PAULESPURY, NORTHANTS.

in 1225. In France there appear to have been wooden effigies at a still earlier date, and the fine figure of Eleanor of Guienne, Queen of Henry II, who died in 1204, is still at Fontevrault, and is believed to be a faithful likeness.

Whether there were many effigies made of stone with heads and hands of oak is doubtful. There may have been a few, and at Towcester Church, Northamptonshire, is an effigy to Archdeacon Sponne, who died in 1448. Before this effigy was needlessly and mischievously " restored " the hands and feet were of wood and the rest of the effigy in stone.[1] Variety of material was sometimes used, and this we know was no uncommon practice on the Continent.

[1] Albert Hartshorne, *Portraiture in Recumbent Effigies*, 35.

PLATE XIX.

Fig. 43.

WALTER DE HELYON (*c.* 1350).   MUCH MARCLE, HEREFORDSHIRE.

Fig. 44.

FOURTEENTH-CENTURY LADY.   LITTLE BADDOW, ESSEX.

Fig. 45.

FOURTEENTH-CENTURY CIVILIAN.   LITTLE BADDOW, ESSEX.

To face page 69.

TOPOGRAPHICAL INDEX

BERKSHIRE

BARKHAM (St. James). In a recess in the east wall of a modern porch.

PERSON REPRESENTED. ? Anne, dau. and heiress of Thomas Nevill, mar. Gilbert, son of Robert Bullock, living 1336.

EFFIGY (5 ft. 1 in. present length) in loose kirtle with tight sleeves, mantle, wimple and veil falling to shoulders, hands in prayer, face and feet destroyed, and head on two cushions. Very good work.

REFERENCES. *Notes and Queries*, 1st S., VIII, 255; *Memoirs of Bullock Family*, 10, 11; *Berks, Bucks and Oxon Arch. Jour.*, V, 81; *Archæologia*, LXI, 512, 521.

BURGHFIELD (St. Mary the Virgin). In the old church in north side of chancel and in new church in vestibule.

PERSON REPRESENTED. Unknown knight.

EFFIGY (6 ft. 6 in., left side cut away) in mail hauberk and hose and coif of mail, over which is a head-piece. Gambeson shows 2 in. below hauberk. Surcoat long and girdle hidden beneath. Left leg crossed over right. Only hilt of sword remains. Head on one cushion supported by angels (one destroyed); feet on lion. Excellent work, and the Westminster angels at head and lion at feet indicate that this figure was carved in a London atelier about the year 1310. See Plate VII, Fig. 17.

REFERENCES. Ashmole's *Antiqs. of Berks*, I, 29; Gough, I, xcix; Lysons *Mag. Brit.*, I, 210; *Notes and Queries*, 1st S., VIII, 255; Prior and Gardner's *Medieval Figure-Sculpture in England*, 668, Fig. 750; *Archæologia*, LXI, 505, 521; *Notes on the Brasses and Effigies at Burghfield, Berkshire*, by I. Chancellor Smith, Trans. Monumental Brass. Soc., 221, illustrated.

ENGLEFIELD (St. Mark). In obtuse wall recess in south aisle.

PERSON REPRESENTED. A lady of the Englefield family, *c.* 1340.

EFFIGY (6 ft. 4 in.). Figure well preserved in long kirtle with tight-fitting sleeves, mantle gathered in plaits at neck, over which is collar (2½ in.), wimple under linen coif, veil falling to shoulders. Head on low cushion; hands in prayer; no support for feet. This tall figure of delicate treatment has been adapted in all probability from an imager's model of a saint. See Plate XVII, Fig. 37.

REFERENCES. Ashmole's *Antiqs. of Berks*, I, 16; Lysons *Mag. Brit.*, I, 209; Gough, I, xcviii; Hollis (illustrated) ; Prior and Gardner's *Medieval Figure-Sculpture in England*, 668 ; *Archæologia*, LXI, 492, 511–512, 521.

SPARSHOLT (Holy Cross). On modern table tomb at west end of Hippisley Chapel.[1]

No. 1. PERSON REPRESENTED. ? Sir Robert Achard.

EFFIGY (6 ft. 10 in. ; hands, arms from elbow, and ends of feet destroyed) in conical bascinet with camail, jupon, hauberk, brassarts, articulated shoulder-pieces, elbow-cops, thigh-pieces, knee-cops, jambs, sollerets, spurs (destroyed) and straps, baudrick (2 in.). Head on helmet with mutilated crest ; feet on lion.

REFERENCES. Leland's *Itinerary of Berks* ; Hollis (illustrated) ; Gough, I, xcviii ; Lysons *Mag. Brit.*, I, 209 ; *Notes and Queries*, 1st S., VIII, 255 ; Clark's *Hundred of Wanting*, 176 ; Ashmole's *Ant. of Berks*, I, 206 ; *Berks, Bucks and Oxon Arch. Jour.*, Oct., 1905 ; *Portfolio* (1893), 207 ; *Arch. Journ.*, LXVI, Lady Achard (illustrated), Pl. XXIII, Hollis ; Prior and Gardner's *Medieval Figure-Sculpture in England*, 607, 609 ; *Archæologia*, LXI, 508, 512, 521.

No. 2. PERSON REPRESENTED. ? Joan, first wife of Sir Robert Achard, 1336.

EFFIGY (6 ft. 1 in.) in kirtle with tight-fitting sleeves, mantle, wimple, and veil falling to shoulders. Hands in prayer. Good workmanship and well preserved. Head on two cushions ; the top one supported by two angels ; two plump pet dogs at feet. Effigy made, probably, in London. See Plate XI, Fig. 26.

REFERENCES. See No. 1 Effigy.

No. 3. PERSON REPRESENTED. ? Agnes, second wife of Sir Robert Achard.

EFFIGY (6 ft.) in kirtle with tight-fitting sleeves, mantle, plaited wimple, and close-fitting coif, and veil falling in elegant folds 10 in. below chin. Hands in prayer. Excellent figure, well preserved. Head on two cushions, the top supported by two angels with mutilated wings ; dog at feet. Date *c.* 1340. Effigy most likely came from a London workshop and based on some such figure as the freestone effigy of a " Lady " at Ifield, Sussex. See Plate XIV, Fig. 32.

REFERENCES. See No. 1 Effigy.

BRECKNOCKSHIRE

BRECON (Brecon Cathedral Church).

No. 1. PERSON REPRESENTED. Reginald Breos, Lord of Brecon.

EFFIGY destroyed. Richard Symonds says (1645) " there is the body of a man, cross-legged, a shield on his left arm, very old and decayed."

Churchyard mentions the figure in 1587, but Major Davis in middle of last century speaks of fragments being used by the washerwomen of Brecon.

REFERENCES. Richard Symonds' *Diary*, 1645 ; Churchyard (1587) ; Jones's

---

[1] Ashmole (1719) says it was " a raised monument of wood." Leland says it stood in the middle of the chapel and the knight lay between his two wives.

PLATE XX.

Fig. 46.

FRANKLIN (c. 1350).   EATON-UNDER-HEYWOOD, SHROPSHIRE.

Fig. 47.

CATHERINE STAFFORD, WIFE OF THE SECOND EARL OF SUFFOLK (1415).   WINGFIELD, SUFFOLK.

Brecknock, I, 128 ; II, 34, 59 ; *Arch. Journ.*, XVIII, 75 ; XXXIII, 250 ; *Progress of the Duke of Beaufort through Wales*, by Thomas Dineley, 1684 ; Poole's *Brecknock* ; *Archæologia*, LXII, 515, 517, 521.

No. 2. PERSON REPRESENTED. John Games of Aberbrân.
EFFIGY destroyed.
REFERENCES. See No. 1 Effigy.

No. 3. PERSON REPRESENTED. Ann, first wife of John Games of Aberbrân and dau. of Sir William Vaughan.
EFFIGY destroyed.
REFERENCES. See No. 1 Effigy.

No. 4. PERSON REPRESENTED. William Games.
EFFIGY destroyed.
REFERENCES. See No. 1 Effigy.

No. 5. PERSON REPRESENTED. Second wife of William Games, dau. of Bodenham of Rotherwas.

EFFIGY destroyed.
REFERENCES. See No. 1 Effigy.

No. 6. PERSON REPRESENTED. Thomas Games.
EFFIGY destroyed.
REFERENCES. See No. 1 Effigy.

No. 7. PERSON REPRESENTED. ? Elinor, wife of Thomas Games, dau. of John Morgan of Pen-y-crug, near Brecon.
EFFIGY (5 ft. 6 in.) in gown with tight sleeves and single ruffs at neck and wrists. Petticoat stiff in front, super-tunic open in front to shoulders, plaited and fastened by scarf. Long chain, 2 ft. 7 in. from waist-band ending in pomander. Head in close-fitting French hood ; two gold chains round neck. Hands in prayer ; face and middle portion of arms mutilated. Two cushions under head. Effigy now under west arcade between nave and south aisle.[1] See Plate XXVI, Fig. 59.
REFERENCES. See No. 1 Effigy.

BUCKINGHAMSHIRE

CLIFTON REYNES (St. Matthew). In recess in north wall of Reynes Chapel, but not on original tomb.
No. 1. PERSON REPRESENTED. ? Sir Ralph Reynes, 1310. This effigy was long attributed to Sir Simon Borard, but he died in 1267.
EFFIGY (5 ft.) in mail coif with fillet, hauberk showing gambeson beneath, mail hose, short surcoat to knees caught up over belt, knee-cops, spurs (gone) and straps. Sword in plain belt hanging obliquely from right hip and fastened in front with plain buckle. Right hand sheathing sword, left holding scabbard. Right leg crossed over left. Moustaches. Dog at feet, and two low cushions under

---

[1] The only remaining figure of a tomb of " three tiers of oaken beds," which stood in the chancel to the memory of John, William, and Thomas Games of Aberbrân. The parliamentarian soldiers destroyed all the figures except this one. Tomb removed in early years of nineteenth century.

head. Figure in good preservation and effigy made locally and was most likely a reproduction of the Totternhoe stone "knights." See Plate VIII, Fig. 18.

REFERENCES. Lysons *Mag. Brit.*, 490; Lipscomb, IV, 120; *Notes and Queries*, 1st S., VIII, 455; MS. *Hist. of Clifton Reynes*, by Rev. Edward Cooke (1821); *Arch. Journ.*, XI, 149 (illustrated); *Bucks Arch. Soc.*, VI, 399; *Notes and Queries*, 6th S., IX, 11; *Portfolio* (1893), 207; Prior and Gardner's *Medieval Figure-Sculpture in England*, 667, Fig. 749; Crossley's *English Church Monuments* (illustrated), 211; *Archæologia*, LXI, 501, 505, 506, 511, 523.

No. 2. PERSON REPRESENTED. ? Wife of Sir Ralph Reynes. Either Amabel, dau. of Sir Henry Green of Broughton (first wife), or Amabel, dau. of Sir Richard Chamberlain of Petso Manor (second wife).

EFFIGY (4 ft. 10 in.) in kirtle with tight-fitting sleeves, and long sleeveless cote-hardie, wimple, and long veil falling to shoulders. Hands in prayer and feet in somewhat pointed shoes. Dog at feet and two low cushions under head. Figure well preserved and effigy of local type. See Plate VIII, Fig. 18.

REFERENCES. See No. 1 Effigy.

No. 3. PERSON REPRESENTED. ? Knight of the Reynes family, *c.* 1330.

EFFIGY (5 ft. 5 in.) in mail coif with skull-cap under, hauberk showing gambeson, mail hose, short sleeveless surcoat with an embattled border, knee-cops, but no spurs or straps. Indication of broad sword-belt, but sword lost. Right leg crossed over left. Right hand broken, doubtless sheathing sword; right arm holds semi-cylindrical heater-shaped shield (1 ft. 7 in. by 1 ft. 1½ in.). Face clean-shaven. Figure in good preservation and effigy made locally. On table-tomb under the western of the two arches separating chancel from Reynes Chapel.[1] See Plate XII, Fig. 28.

REFERENCES. See No. 1 Effigy.

No. 4. PERSON REPRESENTED. Wife of the above knight, *c.* 1330.

EFFIGY (5 ft. 6 in.) in kirtle with tight-fitting sleeves, sleeveless cote-hardie without girdle, cut low at neck, wimple, veil falling to shoulders with fillet encircling temples and another passing from forehead over the crown. Feet small, hands in prayer. Dog (mutilated) at feet, two low cushions under head. Figure well preserved and of local type. See Plate XII, Fig. 28.

REFERENCES. See No. 1 Effigy.

CAMBRIDGESHIRE

HILDERSHAM (Holy Trinity). Under arch between chancel and south chapel (now organ chamber) on modern tomb.

No. 1. PERSON REPRESENTED. Lysons conjectured this effigy was that of Sir Thomas Busteler; but he died 1370, and this figure is of an earlier date.

---

[1] This tomb, decorated with shields of arms, may not belong to these effigies, as fragments of a table-tomb were found in the middle of the Reynes Chapel.

EFFIGY (6 ft.) in mail hauberk and hose, mail coif, knee-cops, straps and spurs (pricks gone), sleeveless surcoat to below knees fastened with cingulum. Right leg crossed over left, right hand sheaths sword, left hand held scabbard. Sword-belt 2 in., but sword broken. Only one foot remains. Lion at feet ; two low cushions under head. Figure repaired and effigy probably made in London. See Plate V, Fig. 12.

REFERENCES. Lysons *Mag. Brit.*, II, 211 ; *Notes and Queries*, 1st S., VIII, 255 ; *Portfolio* (1893), 207 ; Kerrich Col. Brit. Mus. drawings, 6730, pp. 27, 28 ; Prior and Gardner's *Medieval Figure-Sculpture in England*, 664 ; *Archæologia*, LXI, 505, 511, 524.

No. 2. PERSON REPRESENTED. ? Wife of the above knight.

EFFIGY (5 ft. 10 in.) in kirtle with tight-fitting sleeves, long cote-hardie to feet, mantle, wimple, and long veil falling to shoulders with narrow fillet round forehead. Hands in prayer. Dog at feet ; two low cushions under head. Board and portions of figure repaired. Effigy now on wooden table-tomb in priest's vestry. See Plate VI, Fig. 13.

REFERENCES. See No. 1 Effigy.

CUMBERLAND

MILLOM (Holy Trinity). On stone tomb at east end of south aisle.

PERSON REPRESENTED. ? Knight of the Huddlestone family, whose ancient stronghold is near the church.

EFFIGY. The lower portion of this figure only remains. Legs straight and encased in thigh-pieces, jambs, and knee-cops, mutilated feet in sollerets. The body is in a jupon with belt (2 in.). Mutilated lion (?) at feet. Length of fragment, 4 ft. 4 in. This fragment was found near to the walled-up west door.

REFERENCES. Lysons *Mag. Brit.*, IV, cxcvi ; *Notes and Queries*, 6th S., VIII, 118 ; Prior and Gardner's *Medieval Figure-Sculpture in England*, 666 ; *Archæologia*, LXI, 508, 525.

OUSBY (St. Luke). On floor of chancel against north wall.

PERSON REPRESENTED. Knight, possibly of either the Falcard or Armstrong families, as the manor of Ousby was divided into moieties between these families in the reign of Henry III, *c.* 1310 to 1320.

EFFIGY (6 ft. 8 in.) in hauberk showing slits at sides and gambeson beneath (4 in.), mail hose, spurs and straps (pricks gone). Camail laced to bascinet through loops decorated with lozenges. Surcoat to below knees fastened with girdle. Narrow sword-belt (1 in.) to which sword was suspended (fragment 1 ft.). Left arm lost, right arm broken at wrist. No shield, but guige passes over right shoulder. Mail on hauberk not set out regularly, but the artist has shown the hose in mail, which is regular and in parallel lines. This fine effigy resembles the knights of Whorlton, Sir John Hastings at Abergavenny, and the third Danbury knight, and was carved, probably, in London. See Plate VIII, Fig. 19.

REFERENCES. Gough, II, cx; Lysons *Mag. Brit.*, IV, cxcvi; *Notes and Queries*, 1st S., VIII, 97; Jefferson's *Hist. of Leath Ward*, 253; Burn, II, 41; Dugd. Bar., I, 566; *Trans. Cumberland and Westmorland Ant. Soc.*, VIII; Prior and Gardner's *Medieval Figure-Sculpture in England*, 666; *Archæologia*, LXI, 501, 525.

ST. BEES.

PERSON REPRESENTED. Anthony, the last Lord Lucy of Egremont. Died 1368.

EFFIGY destroyed. Formerly on south side of the nave. (Hutchinson (1794) says that " the figure is represented in a coat of mail with elevated hands"; Jefferson (1842) speaks of the figure being made of wood and in armour. Bures describes the effigy as being 6 ft. in length. It disappeared during the first half of the nineteenth century.)

REFERENCES. Gough, II, cx; Hutchinson's *Hist. of Cumberland*, II, 41; Nicholson and Burns, 41; Lysons, CXCVII; Jefferson's *Allendale Ward*, 349.

DERBYSHIRE

DERBY (All Saints). At east end of north aisle of chancel.

No. 1. PERSON REPRESENTED. Conjectured to be Robert Johnson, subdean of this collegiate church as late as 1527. He was a great benefactor to the church.

EFFIGY (5 ft. 8½ in.) of a secular canon vested in cassock, surplice, almuce and cope. Mr. W. H. St. John Hope points out that "it shows most admirably the tails forming the fringe of the tippet of the furred almuce, and those on the pendants in front. The addition of a cope is an uncommon feature." Hands in prayer, hair long, falling below ears, and feet in broad-toed shoes. At feet collared hound (conjectural restoration); head on two cushions supported by two reclining angels. South side of tomb has the original carving containing thirteen bede-folk carved in

high relief beneath singular pointed canopies supported on twisted shafts. See Plate XXV, Fig. 57.

REFERENCES. Bassano, a heraldic painter described this tomb in 1710 (MS. College of Arms); Glover's *Hist. of Derby*, II, Pt. i, 495; *Proc. Soc. Ant.*, 2nd S., X, 65 (illustrated); *Derbyshire Arch. and Nat. Hist. Soc.* (Paper on this effigy by Sir William Hope), illustrated, Plate XVII (figure), Plate XVII (front of carved oak tomb), VIII, 185–189; *Portfolio* (1893), 207; *Archæologia*, LXI, 497, 525.

No. 2. PERSON REPRESENTED. See No. 1 Effigy.

EFFIGY (male Cadaver, 2 ft. 10 in.), which has lost one-third of original length, in shroud covering head, but leaving face visible. Girdle round waist. In a recess under above tomb.

REFERENCES. See No. 1 Effigy.

PLATE XXI.

Fig. 48.

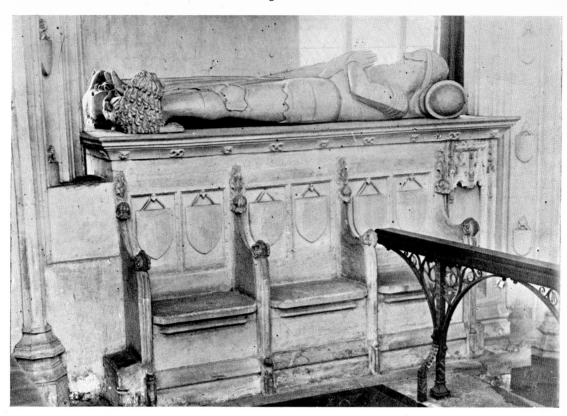

MICHAEL DE LA POLE, SECOND EARL OF SUFFOLK (1415). WINGFIELD, SUFFOLK.

Fig. 49.

DETAIL OF THE WINGFIELD EFFIGIES.

DEVON

TAWSTOCK (St. Peter). In an obtuse recess in the north wall of the chancel.

PERSON REPRESENTED. Unknown "lady."

EFFIGY (4 ft. 4 in. present length), in kirtle with tight-fitting sleeves, long mantle caught up over arms in graceful folds, and fastened by two bands secured by jewelled studs, wimple, coverchief edged with lace falling in graceful folds to shoulders. Hands in prayer. Figure in good condition except for destruction of board and loss of lower portion of body. One oblong cushion under head. Effigy made in Bristol. Date 1330–1340. See Plate XV, Fig. 33.

REFERENCES. *Trans. Exeter Diocesan Architectural Soc.*, VI, 192, 193 (illustrated on Plate XXII); *Worth's Hist. of Devon*, 126; Prior and Gardner's *Medieval Figure-Sculpture in England*, 669; Roger's *Ancient Sepulchral Effigies of Devon*, 365, Pl. III; *Archæologia*, LXI, 512, 26; *Trans. Exeter Diocesan Architectural Soc.*, VI, 192, 193, Plate XXII.

WEST DOWN (Holy Trinity). In arched recess of north wall of north transept.

No. 1. PERSON REPRESENTED. Sir John Stowford (1290 ?–1372 ?), King's Serjeant in 1340, Judge of Court of Common Pleas, 1342 until 1372, except for one month, when (Nov., 1345) Chief Baron of Exchequer. See *Prince's Worthies of Devon*, 559; Dugdale's *Origin*, 45; *Dic. Nat. Biog.*, LV, 8; Foss's *Judges of England*.

EFFIGY (6 ft. 6 in.) in cassock, sleeveless upper gown, tippet pleated at shoulders, and hood falling forward on neck; head mutilated, but doubtless in coif; features quite disfigured. Hands in prayer. Head on one cushion. Effigy made, probably, in Bristol.

REFERENCES. Lysons *Mag. Brit.*, V, cccxxxiii; *Arch. Journ.*, XVIII, 75; Roger's *Ancient Sepulchral Effigies of Devon*, 366, Pl. VI; *Archæologia*, LXI, 496, 526; *Note Book of Tristram Risdon*, 98, 168, 190; *Prince's Worthies of Devon* (1701), 559, 560.

No. 2. PERSON REPRESENTED. Dame Joan, co-heiress of Tracys of Woolocombe, and wife of Sir John Stowford, or Stanford. She and her husband held lands at South Petherton and Drayton, Somerset.

EFFIGY destroyed. Effigy was, probably, made in Bristol.

REFERENCES. See No. 1 Effigy.

COUNTY DURHAM

AUCKLAND (St. Andrew). North-west corner of nave on modern stone tomb.

PERSON REPRESENTED. ? Knight of the Pollard family.

EFFIGY (7 ft. 6 in.) in hauberk with sleeves prolonged to form mittens, hose smooth and possibly painted to indicate plate or leather, bascinet with camail attached showing lacings, spurs (pricks gone) and straps, kneecops, surcoat to knees fastened with girdle, shield lost. Sword-belt (2¾ in.)

and sword on left side. Hands in prayer. Boar at feet ; two cushions under head. The authors of *Medieval Figure-Sculpture in England* consider this effigy is in " style of a reproduction of a stone ' knight ' of *c.* 1340, such as that lying to the south of the passage at Bedale." See Plate XV, Fig. 34.

REFERENCES. Hutchinson's *Durham*, III, 330 ; Pennant's *Tour in Scotland*, III, 314 ; *Arch. Jour.*, XVIII, 74 ; Boyle's *Guide to Durham*, 504 ; *Archæologia Æliana*, XX, 171 ; Prior and Gardner's *Medieval Figure-Sculpture in England*, 666 ; *Archæologia*, LXI, 493, 505, 525.

BRANCEPETH (St. Brandon). Middle of chancel.)[1]

No. 1. PERSON REPRESENTED. Ralph Neville, 2nd Earl of Westmorland, son of John, eldest son of 1st Earl. He died 1484. His only son perished in battle of St. Albans, 1455. See *Dict. Nat. Biog.*, XL, 277.

EFFIGY (6 ft. 3 in.) in complete plate armour, beneath jupon with scalloped edge, hands in prayer, slightly ornamented girdle, sword (only hilt remains) slung by transverse belt, collar of roses, *en soleil* with boar pendant visored salade with chin-piece. At feet dog with collar, and two desks with kneeling figures (destroyed). Head on helm with bull's headcrest supported by three mutilated figures. Good work, and figures of both earl and countess fairly well preserved. See Plate XXII, Fig. 50.

REFERENCES. Leland's *Itin.*, I, 80 ; Hutchinson's *Hist. of Durham*, III, 314 ; Boyle's *Guide to Durham*, 456 ; *Notes and Queries*, 1st S., IX, iii ; illustrated in Billing's *Antiqs. of Durham* ; *Portfolio* (1893), 207 (illustrated) ; Stothard's *Monumental Effigies* (illustrated), Plates 134, 135 ; *Arch. Jour.*, IV, 119 ; Prior and Gardner's *Medieval Figure-Sculpture in England*, 713, Fig. 811 ; Crossley's *English Church Monuments* (illustrated), 217 ; *Archæologia*, LXI, 512, 513, 527.

No. 2. PERSON REPRESENTED. Margaret, Countess of Westmorland, 2nd wife of Ralph Neville, 2nd Earl of Westmorland, dau. of Reginald, Lord Cobham.

EFFIGY (6 ft. 3 in.) in kirtle cut low in front with tight-fitting mitten sleeves, sleeveless surcoat with deep facings most likely of fur, girdle of suns and roses alternately, long mantle fastened by cords attached to ornaments, collar round neck of roses *en soleil* (only five perfect) with lozenge-shaped pendant, head supported by two cushions, steeple head-dress (8 in. high) and veil (1 ft. 10 in.) held up by three figures (mutilated). Hands raised in prayer. At feet are two small dogs ; also desks and figures (destroyed) similar to those at feet of the Earl's effigy. See Plate XXII, Fig. 51.

REFERENCES. See No. 1 Effigy.

DURHAM (St. Giles'). South side of chancel on modern wooden tomb.

---

[1] This tomb has been cut down so that the entablature rests on the base. This was done before Leland saw it.

PERSON REPRESENTED. John Heath of Kepier. The family of Heath acquired the estates of Kepier late in sixteenth century, and resided in house within precincts of dissolved hospital. John Heath and Bernard Gilpin founded the Kepier School of Houghton-le-Spring. Died 1590, and buried in chancel of St. Giles', Durham.

EFFIGY (5 ft.) in pigeon-shaped breast and back plates with scalloped edging of three borders at bottom, gorget of plate having collar with slits and single ruff, shoulder-pieces, brassarts, elbow-cops, vambraces, gauntlets (hands in prayer), thigh-pieces, knee-cops, jambs, sollerets, rowel spurs, sword with twisted hilt suspended by strap over right shoulder, head uncovered, moustaches drooping, beard short and pointed, nose flattened, face long. Figure suffered much in restoration made in 1843. Head on tilting helmet with crest of cock's head attached by a wreath. Feet on scroll (HODIE MICHI above, CRAS TIBI below) enfolding two death's heads (6 in. long). See Plate XXVIII, Fig. 63.

REFERENCES. Fordyce's *Hist. of Durham*, 377; *Memorials of St. Giles', Durham*, Surtees Soc., XCV (1895); Hutchinson's *Hist. of Durham*, II, 303; Boyle's *Guide to Durham*, 383; *Notes and Queries*, 1st S., VIII, 180; *Some Minor Arts*, 66; *Portfolio* (1893), 207; *Archæologia*, LXI, 518, 527.

GREATHAM HOSPITAL.

PERSON REPRESENTED. ? Andrew Stanley, first master of Greatham Hospital. The charter of endowment bears the date 1272.

EFFIGY destroyed. (Gough, II, cx, says there then existed a wooden effigy of a priest in "habit of secular clergyman," cap and end of staff between feet, head on cushion, dog at feet. Figure much defaced, resting "under an arch, probably coeval with the original building." Hutchinson in 1794 also refers to this effigy.)

REFERENCES. Gough, II, cx; *Gent. Mag.*, 1788 (illustrated), 1046, also 1798, 591; Hutchinson's *Hist. of Durham*, III, 91.

STAINDROP (St. Mary the Virgin). South-west corner of south aisle.

No. 1. PERSON REPRESENTED. Henry Neville, 5th Earl of Westmorland, born 1525 and succeeded to title 1550. In 1557 appointed general of horse for northern army. At time of death (1564) he was being tried in the ecclesiastical court for marrying his deceased wife's sister. See *Dict. Nat. Biog.*, XL, 279; *Trans. Durham Arch. Soc.*, IV, 224.

EFFIGY (6 ft. 9 in.) in complete plate armour, gauntlets (hands in prayer), narrow sword-belt (sword lost) suspended on left by three straps, plate gorget adorned with roses. Gold chain with George. Head uncovered, short curls, drooping moustaches, beard divided in two points. Figure well carved is placed between two wives on wooden monument, east end adorned with armorial bearings, west end lost, kneeling figures of the Earl's eight children. (See Plate XXVII, Fig. 61.) Inscription round edge of table states that tomb was made in 1560 for the Earl and his wives, Margaret (3rd wife) and Jane (2nd wife). Head on mutilated crest of bull's head; hound at feet.

REFERENCES. Gough, I, xcix; *Ant. Repertory*, III, 303 (illustrated); Hutchinson's *Hist. of Durham*, III, 261; Boyle's *Guide to Durham*, 708; *Portfolio* (1893), 207; *Trans. Durham Arch. Soc.*, IV, 224; *Archæologia*, LXI, 517, 538.

No. 2. PERSON REPRESENTED. Jane, Countess of Westmorland, 2nd wife of Henry Neville, 5th Earl of Westmorland, dau. of Sir Roger Cholmeley.

EFFIGY (6 ft. 4 in.) in gown, or super-tunic, plaited from waist and open V-shape to show stiff petticoat with ornamental border, sleeves slashed open, fastened with round ornaments, showing tight-fitting under-sleeves, girdle with pomander hung from chain (2 ft. 8 in.). Gold chain with pendant ornament round neck. Partlet, small ruffs at neck and wrists, French cap adorned with Tudor roses and lappet. Hands in prayer. Head on two cushions. Small dog at feet.

REFERENCES. See No. 1 Effigy.

No. 3. PERSON REPRESENTED. Margaret, Countess of Westmorland, third wife of Henry Neville, 5th Earl of Westmorland, widow of Sir Henry Gascoigne, and sister to Earl's second wife.

EFFIGY (6 ft. 7 in.) in gown, or super-tunic, plaited from waist and open V-shape to show stiff petticoat with ornamental border, tight-fitting sleeves adorned with lozenge-shaped pattern and puffs at shoulders decorated with a chevron and bands of needlework below, bodice open at neck, with lappets having edging of Tudor roses, French cap ornamented with Tudor roses and long lappet behind. Gold chain twice encircles neck, having jewel as pendant. Girdle with pomander shaped like a wheel hangs from chain (2 ft. 11 in.). Hands in prayer. Head on two cushions; feet on two small dogs with collars.

REFERENCES. See No. 1 Effigy.

ESSEX

DANBURY (St. John Baptist). Recess in north wall of nave.

No. 1. PERSON REPRESENTED. The three effigies at Danbury are possibly members of the St. Clere family, as they held land in this place from reign of Stephen. The oldest of the three figures was probably carved late in the thirteenth century, the other two belong to the first quarter of the fourteenth century.

EFFIGY (6 ft. 5 in.) in suit of mail coif, hauberk, and hose of mail, long surcoat, girdle, shield-strap (shield lost), sword belt, spurs (pricks broken) and straps. Hands in mail, right sheathing sword, left on scabbard. Left leg crossed over right, and head turned to right shoulder. Head on square cushion. Feet on lion (mutilated). Work good and carved, probably

PLATE XXII.

Fig. 50.

RALPH NEVILLE, SECOND EARL OF WESTMORLAND (DIED 1484).   BRANCEPETH, CO. DURHAM.

Fig. 51.

RALPH NEVILLE, SECOND EARL OF WESTMORLAND, AND MARGARET, HIS WIFE (1484).
BRANCEPETH, CO. DURHAM.

in a London atelier. See Plate III, Fig. 5.

REFERENCES. Weever's *Ancient Funeral Monuments*, 640 ; Gough, I, xcviii, 32 (illustrated), Plate VII, 3 and 4 (drawings by Mr. Tyson) ; *Notes and Queries*, 1st S., VII, 607 ; Weale's *Architectural Papers* ; Morrant's *Essex*, II, 30 ; Durrant's *Essex*, 89 ; Chancellor's *Monuments of Essex* (illustrated), Plates XXXIII and XXXIV ; Suckling's *Essex* (illustrated) ; *Hist. of Essex*, by a Gentleman, I, 188 ; Strutt (illustrated), I, XLV and XLVI ; *Gent. Mag.*, LIX, 337, 338 ; IV, 102 ; *Portfolio* (1893), 207 ; Prior and Gardner's *Medieval Figure-Sculpture in England*, 664, 666, Fig. 747 ; *Archæologia*, LXI, 501, 529.

No. 2. PERSON REPRESENTED. See preceding page.

EFFIGY (6 ft. 8 in.) in suit of mail, coif, hauberk, and hose, long surcoat, girdle, shield-strap (shield lost), sword-belt, spurs (broken) and straps. Hands in mail, right sheathing cross-handled sword and left on scabbard. Left leg crossed over right. Snake coiled round point of sword. Head on square cushion and turned to right shoulder. Feet on lion. Work good and most likely made in London. See Plate V, Fig. 10.

REFERENCES. See No. 1 Effigy.

No. 3. PERSON REPRESENTED. See above.

EFFIGY (6 ft. 6 in.) in suit of mail, coif with fillet round temples, hauberk, mail hose, long surcoat, girdle, shield strap (shield lost), sword-belt (3 in.), sword (hilt broken) on left (2 ft. 10 in.), spurs (pricks gone) and straps. Hands in prayer, left leg crossed over right, head turned to left shoulder. Good work and probably carved in London. In wall recess in south aisle of nave. Wall rebuilt in 1776 when original tomb was destroyed.

REFERENCES. See No. 1 Effigy.

EARL'S COLNE (St. Andrew).

No. 1. PERSON REPRESENTED. ? An Earl of Oxford. Too late for Hugh de Vere, who died 1263. The effigy of Robert, 5th Earl, is supposed to be one now in the cloister. It may be his son Robert, who was buried in the Priory.

EFFIGY destroyed, according to Gough, in 1736.

(Gough gives an illustration of this effigy, from drawing by Daniel King (1653), in coif of mail, with ornamented fillet, hauberk, mail hose, long surcoat, sword-belt with sword on left side, hands in prayer, right leg crossed over left. Dog at feet ; head on cushion supported by two angels. Morant speaks of three cross-legged effigies at Earl's Colne existing in 1768. See Morant's *Essex*, II, 213.)

REFERENCES. Weever, 614 ; Gough, I (illustrations of Earl and Countess) ; Chancellor's *Monuments of Essex* ; *Hist. of Essex*, by a Gentleman (1772), VI, 199 ; Morant's *Essex*, II, 213 ; Wright's *Essex*, I, 424 ; *Archæologia*, LXI, 530.

No. 2. PERSON REPRESENTED. ? A Countess of Oxford.

EFFIGY destroyed according to Gough in 1736.

(Gough's illustration from Daniel King's drawing (1653) shows the lady in wimple, veil with ornamented fillet round temples, kirtle, tight-fitting sleeves, mantle fastened with cords ending in tassels, chain round neck. Hands in prayer, boar at feet, and head on one cushion. Weever mentions this effigy in 1631; but Morant does not speak of it.)
REFERENCES. See No. 1 Effigy.

No. 3. PERSON REPRESENTED. ? Some member of the De Vere family.
EFFIGY destroyed.

(This was a cross-legged effigy with hound at feet. See Weever, 614; Morant's *Essex*, II, 213.)
REFERENCES. See No. 1 Effigy.

No. 4. PERSON REPRESENTED. ? Some member of the De Vere family.
EFFIGY destroyed.

(A cross-legged effigy which Weever says is " quite broken away from his target," and Morant speaks of all three as " much broken and defaced." These effigies were originally in the priory church; but at the suppression were removed to the parish church of St. Andrew.)
REFERENCES. See No. 1 Effigy.

ELMSTEAD (St. Laurence and St. Anne). Ledge of east window of south chapel.
PERSON REPRESENTED. ? Some member of Tony family (1310–15). Family held manor from 1250 to 1317. Mr. Henry Laver, F.S.A., conjectures it to be the effigy of Laurence Tony, 1317.
EFFIGY (6 ft. 11 in.) in suit of mail, helm over coif of mail, hauberk, plates on arms, elbow-cops (with small articulations), surcoat, belt, spurs (pricks damaged) and straps, sword-belt (2¼ in.) shows holes for buckling and holds scabbard (3 ft.). Right arm across breast (hand broken), possibly sheathing sword. Right leg crossed over left. Knight laid on shield (2 ft. by 1 ft. 2 in.). Transitional figure (1310–15) between the simple mail hood and bascinet with attached camail. Head on lion; feet on lap of mutilated figure of civilian in long gown and hood, of which long folds hang down behind (upper portion destroyed).
REFERENCES. Morant's *Essex*, I, 445; *Hist. of Essex*, by a Gentleman (1772), VI, 7; Wright's *Essex*, II, 760; *Arch. Jour.* XVIII, 74; Durrant's *Essex*, 98; Chancellor's *Monuments of Essex* (illustrated), Plate CXXI; *Trans. Essex Arch. Soc.*, X, Part 3 (Elmstead Church); *Archæologia*, LXI, 501, 502, 531.

LITTLE BADDOW (St. Mary the Virgin). Original wall recess in south wall of south aisle.
No. 1. PERSON REPRESENTED. Unknown franklin.
EFFIGY (4 ft. 11 in.) in under-tunic with tight-fitting sleeves, fastened with eighteen buttons, outer cote with wide sleeves to elbows, hair in long curls to neck, face clean-shaven, and hands in prayer. Head on cushion, dog at feet. In poor preservation; hole in lower part of arm and breast. Effigy made locally in fourteenth century and coarsely modelled. See Plate XIX, Fig. 45.

REFERENCES. Gough, I, clvi; *Arch. Jour.*, XVIII, 74; Wright's *Essex*, I, 122; Durrant's *Essex*, 38; Chancellor's *Monuments of Essex* (illustrated), Plate CXXV; *Hist. of Essex*, by a Gentleman, I, 172; Prior and Gardner's *Medieval Figure-Sculpture in England*, 669; *Archæologia*, LXI, 498, 499, 500, 511, 531.

No. 2. PERSON REPRESENTED. Unknown lady. Probably the wife of the above franklin.

EFFIGY (5 ft. 3 in.) in wimple, long veil with fillet round temples, kirtle having tight-fitting sleeves fastened with twenty-four buttons, cotehardie with wide open sleeves, and hands in prayer. Head on two cushions; dog at feet. Figure in poor preservation. Effigy made locally in fourteenth century and coarsely modelled. See Plate XIX, Fig. 44.

REFERENCES. See No. 1 Effigy.

LITTLE HORKESLEY (St. Peter and St. Paul). West end of south chapel, on modern wooden tomb.

No. 1. PERSON REPRESENTED. " Lady " (1290–1300). Possibly wife of Sir William Horkesley, died 1296.

EFFIGY (7 ft. 10 in.) in wimple, long veil with fillet round temples, kirtle, cote-hardie, short mantle to just above knees and caught up over elbows, hands (destroyed) in prayer. Small dog at each foot, tail to tail; cushion for head, with fragments of what may have been supporting angels. Good work and a fine tall, restrained figure of delicate treatment has been adapted in all prob-

ability from an imager's model of a saint. See Plate III, Fig. 7.

REFERENCES. Suckling's *Essex* (illustrated), 103; *Arch. Journ.*, I, 70; *Notes and Queries*, 1st S., VII, 607; Durrant's *Essex*, 128; *Hist. of Essex*, by a Gentleman (1772), VI, 235; *Excursions in Essex*, II, 178 (illustrated); Chancellor's *Monuments of Essex* (illustrated), Plate XXX; *Portfolio* (1893), 207; Prior and Gardner's *Medieval Figure-Sculpture in England*, 664, Fig. 744; *Archæologia*, LXI, 501, 511, 532.

No. 2. PERSON REPRESENTED. ? Knight of the Horkesley family.

EFFIGY (7 ft. 7 in.) in suit of mail, coif with fillet round temples, hauberk, mail hose, knee-cops, ample surcoat with girdle, spurs (pricks gone) and straps, and fragment of broad sword-belt. Right leg crossed over left hands in prayer (destroyed). The hood is concentrically ringed round the face in the early fashion, and the surcoat is open to the waist like effigy of Robert, Duke of Normandy, at Gloucester. Head on low cushion; lion at feet. Date *c.* 1290. This interesting effigy is in a damaged and mutilated state and was probably carved in London. See Plate III, Fig. 6.

REFERENCES. See No. 1 Effigy.

No. 3. PERSON REPRESENTED. ? Knight of the Horkesley family, possibly Sir William Horkesley, 1296.

EFFIGY (7 ft. 10 in.) in suit of mail, coif with fillet round temples, hauberk, mail hose, knee-cops, long surcoat with girdle, spurs (pricks gone) and straps, sword (fragment 2 ft. 2 in.) having hilt with straight quillons, fastened to sword-belt (1¾ in.) slung diagonally, having buckle in front. Hands in prayer clasping, a heart, right leg crossed over left, shield on left arm (fragment 1 ft. 11 in.). Hood concentrically ringed round face in the early fashion. Head on two low cushions; lion at feet. Date *c.* 1290. Effigy probably made in London. See Plate III, Fig. 6.

REFERENCES. See No. 1 Effigy.

LITTLE LEIGHS (St. Laurence and St. Anne). In original wall recess under richly cusped ogee canopy in north wall of chancel.

PERSON REPRESENTED. Unknown ecclesiastic.

EFFIGY (5 ft. 6 in.) in amice (broken in front), alb, oval chasuble, stole, fringed fanon, hair worn long to neck, hands in prayer, head on low cushion

supported by two mutilated angels, at feet a dog in a coat and a hare with long ears ? Date *c.* 1320. See Plate XIII, Fig. 29.

REFERENCES. *Arch. Jour.*, XVIII, 73 ; *Trans. Essex Arch. Soc.*, II, 167 ; Durrant's *Essex*, 144 ; Chancellor's *Monuments of Essex* (illustrated) ; *Archæologia*, LXI, 497, 532.

MESSING (All Saints'). Recess in north wall.

PERSON REPRESENTED. ? Sir William de Messing, founder of the church.

EFFIGY destroyed.

(Cross-legged effigy of knight destroyed by parish clerk at the command of the vicar about one hundred years ago.)

REFERENCES. Gough, I, xcviii ; Suckling's *Essex*, 130 ; *Arch. Journ.*, XVIII ; Walpole (1749) ; *Hist. of Essex*, by a Gentleman (1772), VI, 149 ; Morant's *Essex*, II, 178 ; Durrant's *Essex*, 154 ; Wright's *Essex*, I, 387 ; *Archæologia*, LXI, 533.

GLOUCESTERSHIRE

GLOUCESTER CATHEDRAL CHURCH. In middle of presbytery before high altar.

PERSON REPRESENTED. Attributed to Robert, Duke of Normandy, son of William the Conqueror, died in Cardiff Castle at the age of 80, February, 1135 (see *Dict. Nat. Biog.*, XLVIII, 349).

EFFIGY (5 ft. 10 in.) in hooded hauberk reaching nearly to knees, coronet ornamented with strawberry leaves and fleurs-de-lys fastened by strap passing through mail across forehead and down right side of face, long surcoat open up to middle, shield-strap

but no trace of shield ; right hand grasps handle of sword (3 ft. 4 in.) partly sheathed, sword-belt (1¾ in.) affixed to sheath, thighs and knees in padded trews, lower portion of legs in mail hose, spurs (pricks gone but iron substitutes added) and straps. Right leg crossed over left, eyes open and moustache worn. Cushion under head ; no support for feet. Effigy on oblong chest of fourteenth or fifteenth century adorned with frieze of narrow pointed leaves and round flowers and ten painted shields of arms. Probable date for effigy 1280.

PLATE XXIII.

Fig. 52.

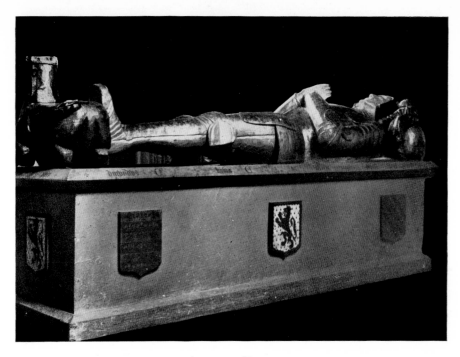

EDMUND CORNEWALL (DIED 1508). BURFORD, SHROPSHIRE.

Fig. 53.

EDMUND CORNEWALL (DIED 1508). BURFORD, SHROPSHIRE.

The peculiarity of the mail on the arms is found on stone effigies at Salisbury, Wareham, Shepton Mallet, Malvern, and statues at Wells and knights at Bristol (1250 to 1280), namely those with surcoat open up to belt like this figure. This effigy was made, probably, in Bristol and is a copy of a mason's " knight " by an imager. In Lansdowne MS. (B.M.) 874, sketch by Lancaster Herald (1610) shows two gold lions on breast of surcoat; and Rev. T. Kerrich's sketch (Kerrich Coll. MS. 6730, p. 21, B.M.) gives surcoat flowered with a four-leaf flower. Effigy broken in Civil War, sold to Sir Humphrey Tracy of Stanway, and mended and replaced at Restoration. See Plate I, Fig. 1.

REFERENCES. Leland's *Itinerary*; Atkyn's *Glos.*, 95; Rudder's *Glos.*, 126; Gough, I, xcvii; *Trans. Bristol and Glos. Arch. Soc.*, XIII, 252, 253; XIV, 238; XXVII, 289–91; *Records of Glos. Cathedral*, I, 99, 101; Lansdowne MS., 874 (B.M.), illustrated; Fosbrooke's *Glos.*; *Gent. Mag.* LIX, Pt. IV, 264; *Portfolio* (1893), 180 (illustrated); Kerrich Coll. MS. 6730, p. 21 (B.M.); Stothart, Pls. 22 and 23; Prior and Gardner's *Medieval Figure-Sculpture in England*, 665, Fig. 745; Crossley's *English Church Monuments*, 181 (illustrated), 209; *Archæologia*, LXI, 493, 494, 495, 499, 500, 501, 533; Bigland's *Glos.*, II (illustrated); Hollis (illustrated); Cox's *Glouc.*, 123.

OLD SODBURY (St. John Baptist). Western recess in north wall of north transept.

PERSON REPRESENTED. ? Knight of the Stephens family, who were buried in the north aisle. This effigy was probably carved near the close of the thirteenth century.

EFFIGY (5 ft. 7 in.) in suit of mail, hauberk reaching to thighs with sleeves covering hands, coif of mail with skull-cap beneath, without supporting strap round forehead being shown, mail hose, surcoat reaching below knees with girdle, no spur-straps or spurs, sword-belt with sword attached (3 ft. 1 in.), an end of belt round scabbard and tag inserted in lower loop, hilt with straight quillons, heater-shaped shield (2 ft. 2 in. by 1 ft. 1 in.) held by enarmes on left arm. Right leg crossed over left, right hand (mutilated) on pommel (?), left holds scabbard. Figure in poor state of preservation; right hand and arm nearly worn away; features destroyed. Date *c.* 1290. Effigy made, most likely, in Bristol.

REFERENCES. Rudder's *Glos.*, 678 (incorrectly speaks of effigy as made of stone); Atkyn's *Glos.*, 355; *Trans. Bristol and Glos. Arch. Soc.*, XXX, 136, 137; *Archæologia*, LXI, 334.

HAMPSHIRE

Monks Sherborne Priory (St. Mary and St. John). Arched recess in south wall of nave (not original tomb).

Person Represented. Some authorities conjecture it is effigy of Sir John de Port, knight, son of Sir Henry de Port, knight, founder of Monks Sherborne Priory (see *Dict. Nat. Biog.*, XLVI, 163). The date, however, is too early, the effigy being *c.* 1310.

Effigy (6 ft.) in suit of mail, hauberk, coif, and hose, surcoat reaching below knees, knee-cops, spurs and straps, cinqulum ($\frac{1}{2}$ in.), guige ($1\frac{1}{4}$ in.), but no shield, sword-belt (2 in.) with sword (2 ft. 2 in.) attached, having hilt with straight quillons. Hands in prayer, lion at feet, and two cushions under head, *c.* 1310. Good work; probably carved by sculptor of effigies of William Combmartin (Alderton) and John Hastings (Abergavenny). See Plate VI, Fig. 14.

References. *Trans. Newbury Field Club*, III, 118; *Archæologia*, LXI, 501, 534.

Thruxton (Holy Rood and St. Peter and St. Paul).

Person Represented. ? Lady Elizabeth Philpotts. The Philpotts held the manor of Thruxton after the Lisles.

Effigy (5 ft. 5 in.) in tight plain gown, long-waisted with straight and formal stomacher with invected edging, tight sleeves, farthingale puffs and petticoat over hips, bodice cut square at neck with ruff, tight-fitting jewelled French cup with long pendant lappets attached falling behind head. Hands destroyed. No support for feet; head on two cushions with geometrical pattern intended for lace. Figure in poor preservation. Replaced in the church, having been in the rector's barn for many years. Mr. Wm. Dale believes this effigy formerly stood where the organ is now placed. See Plate XXVIII, Fig. 64.

References. *Trans. Salisbury Field Club*, I, 187; *Proc. Soc. Ant. Lond.*, 2nd S., XXII, 251; *Archæologia*, LXI, 518, 534.

ISLE OF WIGHT

Brading (St. Mary the Virgin). On table-tomb, south side of Oglander Chapel.

No. 1. Person Represented. Sir William Oglander, knighted 1606, married Ann, daughter of Anthony Dillington of Knighton. Died 1608 (see *Dict. Nat. Biog.*, XLII, 34).

Effigy (6 ft. 1 in.) in plate armour engraved with herring-bone pattern,

breast and back plates showing hinges, five taces, thigh-pieces, jambs, knee-cops, sollerets, rowel spurs, plate gorget, shoulder-pieces, brassarts, vambraces, and elbow-cops. Hands bare and in prayer, holding heart, head uncovered, features well sculptured, beard trimmed, moustaches slightly drooping. Sword (3 ft. 9 in.) suspended from belt, has pommel adorned with woman's face. Figure well executed and carved at Newport (Isle of Wight) between 1625 and 1640, for £33. See Plate XXIX, Fig. 65.

REFERENCES. Oglander MS.; Worsley's *Isle of Wight*, 194; Stone's *Architectural Ant. Isle of Wight*, I, 15 (illustrated); Englefield, 96; Barber's *Guide Isle of Wight* (1850), 28, 29; *Notes and Queries*, 1st S., IX, 17; *Arch. Journ.*, XXXIII, 242; *Archæologia*, LXI, 493, 500, 519, 535.

No. 2. PERSON REPRESENTED. Sir John Oglander, born 1585, knighted 1615, Deputy-Governor of the Isle of Wight 1624, sat for several Parliaments. Exhibited zeal in Royalist cause and adhered to Charles I at outbreak of Civil War. Died 1655, and portion of his valuable *Diary* was published in 1888 (see *Dict. Nat. Biog.*, XLII, 34).

EFFIGY (6 ft. 2 in.) in plate armour adorned with scroll pattern, breast and back plates, three taces with tuilles hinged to the bottom tace, thigh-pieces, jambs, knee-pieces, sollerets, rowel spurs, large engrailed shoulder-pieces, brassarts, elbow-cops, vambraces. The figure lies on right side, right hand supports head, right leg crossed over left, left hand holds hilt of sword (3 ft. 6 in.) having hilt with twisted quillons and ornamented pommel; sheath suspended by strap to belt (1 in.) fastened by a locket. Hands bare, on left arm shield (*à bouche* 1 ft. 9 in. by 1 ft. 5 in.) charged with Oglander arms (azure a stork between three cross-crosslets fitchy or). Head in helmet with visor raised showing face

with moustaches and top of beard. Figure badly executed, legs clumsy, right arms out of proportion, only measuring 7 in. from elbow to wrist. On table-tomb, north side of Oglander Chapel. See Plate XXIX, Fig. 66.

REFERENCES. See No. 1 Effigy.

No. 3. PERSON REPRESENTED. George Oglander, only son of Sir John Oglander, knight, who died of smallpox at Caen, in Normandy, during a tour made on his coming of age.

EFFIGY. This diminutive figure (1 ft. 9 in.) is an exact copy of the effigy of Sir John Oglander, except that the feet have no spurs, the sword is curved near the point, and the features are those of a young man.

These three effigies were repainted about 50 years ago. Sir John Oglander's will (dated 10th November, 1649) left instructions for his executors to place the effigy of his father on south side of chapel, and his own effigy on north side. This effigy was already made, and the testator was so well pleased with it that he ordered his executors to make a small replica of it for his son George. In plain round-headed wall recess in north wall of Oglander Chapel above tomb of Sir John Oglander. See Plate XXIX, Fig. 66.

REFERENCES. See No. 1 Effigy.

GATCOMBE (St. Olive). Round-headed recess in north wall of chancel.

PERSON REPRESENTED. If the effigy be genuine it may be a member of the Estur family, who owned the manor of Gatcombe from time of Domesday to Edward II.

EFFIGY (5 ft. 11 in.) in mail hauberk

and hose, long surcoat, cingulum, guige (2 in.) supports uncharged, heater-shaped shield (1 ft. 6 in. by 1 ft. 6 in.). Head (later restoration) in salade; right hand holds pommel of sword (fragment 1 ft. 2 in.) which is attached to belt (1½ in.) on left side. Head on round cushion supported by two angels (one mutilated —the other with restored head and neck); animal (? otter) at feet. Figure has no merit, and it is doubtful if any portion is of great antiquity; probable that the whole work is an anachronism which may be assigned to the Jacobean period.

REFERENCES. Worsley's *Isle of Wight*, 186; Stone's *Architectural Ant. Isle of Wight*, II, 25 (illustrated); *Archæologia*, LXI, 494, 496, 536.

HEREFORDSHIRE

ABBEY DORE.

PERSON REPRESENTED. Cadwgan, Bishop of Bangor (1215–36) for twenty years; obtained permission from Pope Gregory IX to retire and become a monk of Dore, where he died 4th November, 1241. See *Dict. Nat. Biog.*, VIII, 194.

EFFIGY destroyed.

(Leland states: *Caducanus sum tyme Byshope of Bangor, after Monke of Dour.* Gibson (1727) quotes Leland and adds: *Of whom I suppose there remains in the South-Isle an almost entire effigy, made of the Heart of Oak! Nothing being either decay'd or broken, but the Top of his Pastoral Staff.* The Hill MSS. (Vol. III, 228) at Belmont shows rough sketch of figure (1716) in gown with large sleeves and hood open at neck and cap on head; left hand holds a cross staff with end thrust in mouth of lion at feet, and maniple (?) on left arm, while right hand holds a book, or possibly a mirror, as Leland says: Cadwgan wrote the "Speculum Christianorum." Mr. George Marshall, in his paper on "Wooden Monumental Effigies in Herefordshire" (*Trans. Woolhope Naturalists Field Club*, 1920), draws attention to Biographical Memories of the Rev. Sneyd Davies, D.D., by George Hardinge, where an expostulatory poem (1816) says effigy sent by Dr. Milles to Lord Bateman in London (1st Viscount died 1744, 2nd Viscount in 1802). As first Viscount was created 1731 and Dr. Davies died 1769, the effigy must have left Abbey Dore between these dates, and although Gough published *Sepulchral Monuments* 1786 he repeats Gibson's statement.)

REFERENCES. Leland, VIII, 86b; Gough, I, 195; *Archæologia*, LXI, 537; "Wooden Monumental Effigies in Herefordshire," by George Marshall, F.S.A. (*Trans. Woolhope Nat. Field Club*, 1920). Sketch in the Hill MSS. is reproduced in this paper.

CLIFFORD (St. Mary the Virgin). In recess in south wall of chancel.

PERSON REPRESENTED. ? Rector of Clifford (1270–80).

EFFIGY (5 ft. 11 in.) in amice, alb, chasuble (3 ft. 10 in.), stole, and

PLATE XXIV.

Fig. 54.

SIR ROGER ROCKLEY (DIED 1522).   WORSBOROUGH, YORKS.

Fig. 55.

SIR ROGER ROCKLEY (DIED 1522).   WORSBOROUGH, YORKS.

fanon, hands in prayer, eyes open, feet in pointed shoes resting on moulded pediment, head on cushion (decayed), bracket at feet. Cut of hair and folds and length of chasuble resemble effigies of Bishop Aquablanca at Hereford (died 1268) and Bishop Bronescombe at Exeter (died 1280). The chasuble is later than those of effigies of 1225–50, but earlier than those displaying the greater fullness and folds of 1290. Good work, well preserved, and effigy made probably in Hereford. See Frontispiece.

REFERENCES. *Arch. Journ.*, XVIII, 75; Harl. MS. 6725; Prior and Gardner's *Medieval Figure-Sculpture in England*, 662, Fig. 741; Crossley's *English Church Monuments* (illustrated), 193; Marshall's "Wooden Monumental Effigies in Herefordshire" (*Trans. Woolhope's Naturalists' Field Club*), illustrated; *Archæologia*, LXI, 496, 536.

MUCH MARCLE (St. Bartholomew). On most easterly window-ledge of north aisle.

PERSON REPRESENTED. Walter de Helyon, franklin, living 1357; made over the Marcle property to only dau. Joan in 1348. She mar. Richard Walwyn.

EFFIGY (6 ft. 4 in.) in long close-fitting cote-hardie, buttoned in front, reaching to knees, with tight-fitting sleeves, buttoned from elbows to wrists. The hood is worn about neck and front of breast, but not drawn over head. Over hips is a girdle (1½ in.) with long pendant and small pouch buckled to it. Close-fitting hose, right leg crossed over left, shoes pointed, bare hands in prayer, face long, short beard and moustaches, hair parted in middle, falling in waves to neck; head on cushion; feet on lion with tail curled round the right foot. Excellent figure, tall, slim, and clean-cut. Mr. Bloxam dates the figure 1350; Mr. Albert Hartshorne conjectures 1360. Cross-legged effigies of civilians are rare; there is one in Thurlaston Church, Leicestershire, and another at Birkin, near Normanton. Effigy made locally, most likely in Hereford. See Plate XIX, Fig. 43.

REFERENCES. Gough, II, cxi; *Arch. Jour.*, XVIII, 75; XXXIII, 239; *Trans. Woolhope Club* (1899), 98; *Antiquary* (1894), 140; *Ass. Arch. Societies*, XII (1873–74); *Trans. Bristol and Gloucs. Arch. Soc.*, XVIII, Pl. i (effigies of civilians) (illustrated, but hood wrongly shown as drawn over the head); Prior and Gardner's *Medieval Figure-Sculpture in England*, 662, Fig. 741; Marshall's "Wooden Monumental Effigies in Herefordshire" (*Trans. Woolhope Naturalists' Field Club*) (illustrated); Crossley's *English Church Monuments* (illustrated), 199; Cooke's continuation of Duncumb's *History of Herefordshire* (illustrated); *Archæologia*, LXI, 498, 499, 537.

HERTFORDSHIRE

AYOT ST. LAURENCE.
PERSON REPRESENTED. Unknown cross-legged knight in mail.
EFFIGY destroyed.

(Gough quotes Mr. Grose, who says that there is in this church a diminutive wooden effigy of a cross-legged knight which on account of its size was called *The Boy Templar*. This fourteenth-century church has been a ruin for 130 years.)
REFERENCES. Gough, II, cix.

HUNTINGDONSHIRE

KEYSTONE.
PERSON REPRESENTED. Cadaver of an unknown ecclesiastic.
EFFIGY. Male cadaver in open shroud approaching a skeleton, thick neck, small tonsured head, straight hair covering ears, figure damaged, right arm and foot lost. Board much decayed, but vestiges of red colour are visible on upper end.

This cadaver has probably been originally placed beneath an effigy of a priest in a position like the one on the tomb to Sir Roger Rockley, ob. 1522, Worsborough, Yorks (Figs. 54 and 55), or Robert Johnson, secular canon, ob. 1527, All Saints', Derby (Fig. 57).

KENT

CANTERBURY CATHEDRAL CHURCH. North wall of Martyrdom, on original table-tomb.
PERSON REPRESENTED. John Peckham, Archbishop of Canterbury, succeeded Archbishop Kilwardby in 1278, died 1292. See *Dict. Nat. Biog.*, XLIV, 190.
EFFIGY (7 ft. 4 in.) in amice, alb, stole, tunicle, dalmatic, chasuble, pall, mitre, gloves, and pointed shoes. Hands in prayer. Head on two cushions; at feet a (?) lion. Fine work; left hand and mitre mutilated and some portions of figure on the left side. Effigy made probably in a London workshop, c. 1290. The tomb on which the effigy lies is decorated with nine niches containing figures of bishops, and stands beneath a finely carved cinquefoiled double cusped arch. See Plate IV, Figs. 8 and 9.
REFERENCES. Gough, I, xci; Woolnoth's *Canterbury*, 85; Somner's *Canterbury*, 256; *Archæologia Cantiana*, XX, 288; *Canterbury Cathedral*, G.S., 105 (illustrated), Plate 7; Dart's *Canterbury Cathedral*, 136 (illustrated); Prior and Gardner's *Medieval Figure-Sculpture in England*, 662, Fig. 740; *Archæologia*, LXI, 497, 501, 537.

GOUDHURST (St. Mary the Virgin). Wooden table-tomb (original) on south side of south aisle, under an oriel window of four lights.
No. 1. PERSON REPRESENTED. Sir Alexander Culpeper, knight (died 1537).

EFFIGY (5 ft. 6 in.) in plate armour, ornamented with scroll-work, cuirass, shoulder-pieces, brassarts, plain elbow-cops, vambraces, thigh-pieces, elaborate articulated knee-cops, jambs, and sabbatons. Hands in prayer, sword (2 ft. 5 in.) on left side, mail gorget (1¾ in.), gold chain round neck, and tabard (now flowered with red pattern). Ends of tuilles beneath tabard richly ornamented with scroll work. Hair long, falling to neck, and face clean-shaven. Head on helmet adorned with oak leaves placed on cushion; smooth-skinned dog at feet. Well preserved and good work. See Plate XXVI, Fig. 58.

REFERENCES. Gough, I, xcix; *Gent. Mag.* (1785), 679; *Archæologia*, LXI, 493, 514, 515, 537.

No. 2. PERSON REPRESENTED. Constance Agnes, dau. of Sir Roger Davis of Northfleet, and wife of Sir Alexander Culpeper.

EFFIGY (5 ft. 4 in.) in dark green petticoat, waistcoat cut square at neck, with attached sleeves having wide wristbands (4 in.), super-tunic fastened across breast with golden band (11 in.) held by gold ornaments, and wide hanging sleeves lined with fur. Feet in broad-toed shoes, hands in prayer, pedimental head-dress adorned with gold band, necklace with pendant and five gold chains, and golden girdle with tassels. Two cushions under head; dog at feet. Figure in good preservation. Both effigies were repainted forty years ago.

REFERENCES. See No. 1 Effigy.

LINCOLNSHIRE

MARKET DEEPING (St. Guthlac).
PERSON REPRESENTED. Sir Baldwin Wake (died 1282).
EFFIGY destroyed, formerly on south side of chancel.

(Exhibited in mail, cross-legged; disappeared before 1782.)
REFERENCES. Gough, II, cx.

MIDDLESEX

WESTMINSTER ABBEY CHURCH.
No. I. PERSON REPRESENTED. Henry V. Born 1387, succeeded his father Henry IV in 1413. Died 1422. See *Dict. Nat. Biog.*, XXVI, 43.
EFFIGY (5 ft. 4 in. present length) is a wooden figure, being the foundation for metal plates. The silver head and plates were stolen in 1546. The thieves also removed the silver plates with name and title and distich DUX

NORMANNORUM VERUS CONQUESTOR EORUM—HERES FRANCORUM DECESSIT ET HECTOR EORUM. Dart's *Westminster* gives illustration showing effigy in tunic and mantle with hands holding sceptre and orb. Two cushions under head; lion at feet. Queen Katherine, widow of Henry V, presented the effigy. On original table-tomb on platform east of the shrine of Edward the Confessor.

REFERENCES. Gough, I, xcix ; Dart's *Westminster* (illustrated), II, 36, 38 ; Stanley's *Westminster Abbey*, 148 ; Smith's *Roll Call of Westminster Abbey*, 66 ; Bradley's *Annals of Westminster Abbey*, 102 ; *Some Minor Arts*, 58 ; *Portfolio* (1893), 180 ; Prior and Gardner's *Medieval Figure-Sculpture in England*, 670 ; *Archæologia*, LXI, 491, 538.

No. 2. PERSON REPRESENTED. William of Valence, titular Earl of Pembroke, fourth son of Isabel of Angoulême, widow of King John, by her second husband, Hugh X of Lusignan, Count of La Marche. His half-brother, Henry III, invited him to England ; but his alien origin, rich marriage, pride and violence involved him in unpopularity. He died at Bayonne (1296), and his remains were buried in Westminster Abbey. See *Dict. Nat. Biog.*, LXI, 373.

EFFIGY (5 ft. 7 in.) is a wooden figure covered with metal plates and Limoges enamelled work on copper gilt. Clad in mail hauberk reaching to middle of thighs, with long sleeves and gambeson beneath, mail hose ; spurs have been fastened with cloth to form straps of extraordinary thickness ; surcoat powdered with escutcheons bearing arms of Valence (only three remain), coif of mail with richly jewelled fillet round temples (empty collets once contained stones or glass), sword on left side (1 ft. 8 in. remaining), shield (1 ft. 8½ in. by 1 ft. 1 in.), borne on left hip, with arms of Valence (*Barry silver and azure an orle of martlets gules*), and hands in prayer. Head on enamelled cushion adorned with quatrefoils and arms of England ; lion at feet. Figure rests on a wooden chest originally adorned with figures and escutcheons (nineteen of these lost escutcheons are engraved in Stothard's *Monumental Effigies*). The chest rests on stone tomb of English work, with shields of England, William of Valence, and of Aymer, his son, dimidiated with those of Clermont. The metallic part of tomb, mode of wearing shield on hip, and decorating of surcoat with little escutcheons, indicate French workmanship. Effigy on north side of Chapel of St. Edmund in south ambulatory. See Plate I, Fig. 2.

REFERENCES. Gough, I, xcviii, 75 (illustrated), Plate XXVII ; Stothard, 41 (illustrated with three plates) ; *Notes and Queries*, 6th S., VII, 451 ; 1st S., VIII, 180 ; Dart's *Westminster*, I, 119 ; *Some Minor Arts*, 58 ; head figured in Doyle's *Official Baronage*, III, 8 ; *Portfolio* (1893), 179 ; Prior and Gardner's *Medieval Figure-Sculpture in England*, 670 ; *Archæologia*, LXI, 491, 499, 539 ; Crossley's *English Church Monuments*, 26 (illustrated).

MONMOUTHSHIRE

ABERGAVENNY (St. Mary's Priory Church). At west end of Herbert Chapel on wooden stand.

PERSON REPRESENTED. John Hastings, second Baron Hastings (eighth by tenure) and Baron Bergavenny (1262–

PLATE XXX.

PLATE XXV.

Fig. 56.

SIR JOHN SAVILLE (DIED 1529) AND WIVES.   THORNHILL, YORKS.

Fig. 57.

? ROBERT JOHNSON, SECULAR CANON (*c.* 1527).   ALL SAINTS', DERBY.

1313), was son of Henry Hastings, first Baron Hastings, and Joan Cantelupe. Buried in church of Friars Minors at Coventry, but effigy is at Abergavenny. See *Dict. Nat. Biog.*, XXV, 130 ; Nicholson's *Roll of Cærlaverock.*

EFFIGY (6 ft. 7 in.) in mail coif with narrow fillet (¼ in.), hauberk, mail hose, knee-cops, spurs (pricks gone) and straps, long surcoat with girdle hanging 10 in. below buckle, sword-belt (2¾ in.), over which portion of surcoat is looped, on right side, and sword (11 in. remains) on left side. Left leg crossed over right ; bare hands in prayer ; head on two cushions ; and lion (defaced) at feet. Good work, and face probably a portrait. Effigy most likely made in a London atelier. See Plate X, Fig. 23.

REFERENCES. Gough, I, xcix ; Coxe, 192 ; Morgan's *Monuments of Abergavenny* (illustrated), Plate I ; Richard Symonds MS., 1645 ; Churchyard's *Worthies of Wales* ; *Notes and Queries*, 6th S., VII, 451 ; Bradney's *Monmouthshire*, 164 (illustrated) ; Prior and Gardner's *Medieval Figure-Sculpture in England*, 666, Fig. 746 ; Crossley's *English Church Monuments*, 181 (illustrated), 212 ; *Archæologia*, LXI, 493, 499, 503, 539.

NORFOLK

BANHAM (St. Mary the Virgin). In modern recess in south wall of chancel.

PERSON REPRESENTED. Unknown knight (1310–20). Blomefield and Gough think it may be the effigy of Sir Hugh Bardolph, Lord of the Manor of Banham ; but he died in 1203.

EFFIGY (6 ft. 1 in.) in close-fitting coif of mail over which is head-piece, hauberk, mail hose, knee-cops, mail gloves divided for fingers, spurs fastened to leather buckled to the top of instep (necks which seem to have been pinned on are lost), short surcoat reaching just below hauberk, girdle and sword-belt (1½ in.). Right hand on right side holds sword. (A sketch was made by Rev. T. Kerrich, and he describes the colour he saw upon this effigy before it was painted and sanded to represent stone.) Head on one cushion ; no support for feet. Two small holes in left arm show there was originally a shield. The original tomb still exists as a wall recess in north aisle of nave.

REFERENCES. Gough, I, xcviii, 36 ; Blomefield's *Norfolk*, I, 240 (illustrated) ; *Notes and Queries*, 1st S., VIII, 19, 179 ; *Portfolio* (1893), 204 ; Kerrich MS. Coll. (B.M.), 6728, pp. 25, 26 ; 6732, p. 13 ; 6730, pp. 13 to 20 (these drawings give details of this effigy as seen in 1779. Mr. Kerrich says that the mail on the legs was formed into squares) ; *Archæologia*, LXI, 493, 505, 540.

FERSFIELD (St. Andrew). In wall recess in south wall of south chapel.

PERSON REPRESENTED. Sir Robert du Bois, knight, son of Sir Robert du Bois, Lord of the Manor, died 1311. Married Christian, dau. of Sir William Latimer.

EFFIGY (6 ft. 1 in.) in hauberk, close-fitting coif of mail over which is a head-piece, mail hose, spurs and spur-straps with device at end of strap, surcoat reaching below knees, cingulum, gloves, sword-belt (1¾ in.), sword (2 ft. 10½ in.), hilt with straight quillons, and scabbard embellished with devices (lost); other devices (lost) were let into the board. See full description of colour and devices in Blomefield's *Norfolk*. Two cushions under head, a buck couchant ermine, crest of du Bois, at feet. Sir Robert du Bois died in 1311, yet this effigy is an instance of the straight-legged attitude, and it is possible that it may not have been carved until the middle of the fourteenth century when this peculiarity again made its appearance. This figure was probably carved in a London workshop. See Plate IX, Figs. 20 and 21.

REFERENCES. Blomefield's *Norfolk*, I, 104 (illustrated); Gough, I, 79 (illustrated), I, xcviii; Stothard (illustrated), Pl. 57; *Notes and Queries*,

1st S., VIII, 19; *Portfolio* (1893), 181; Kerrich MS. Coll. (B.M.), 6730, pp. 83, 84; 6731, p. 24 (these drawings show the effigy and details of armour); *Archæologia*, LXI, 493, 504, 540.

SOUTHACRE (St. George). In wall recess in south wall of chancel.

PERSON REPRESENTED. ? Knight of Harsick family; possibly Sir Alexander Harsick, and not, as Gough says, "the first of that surname."

EFFIGY (4 ft. 3 in. fragment) with head uncovered, hair long, gorget, jupon, baudrick and knee-cops. The present fragment is sadly mutilated and shows only head, trunk, and 6 in. of the right leg. The drawing by the Rev. T. Kerrich, made 1779, shows it was then less mutilated. The jupon indicates that the effigy might be dated between 1340 and 1413.

REFERENCES. Blomefield's *Norfolk*, III, 418; Weever, f. 815; Gough, I, xcviii; Kerrich MS. Coll., 6730, p. 61 (B.M.); *Archæologia*, LXI, 540.

NORTHAMPTONSHIRE

ALDERTON (St. Margaret). Originally in south aisle, removed to belfry in 1848, but now replaced in the church.

PERSON REPRESENTED. Sir William Combmartin. Alderton and other manors passed by Maud, the only daughter of Patrick, last of the Chaworths, who conveyed them to William Combmartin. He was certified as lord of these places 1315, and in 1318 custody of manors and wardship of his three daughters were granted to Margaret, his widow. See Hartshorne's *Northants Effigies*, 92.

EFFIGY (6 ft. 4 in.) in coif of mail with studded fillet round temples, hauberk, mail hose, surcoat reaching below knees with cingulum (¾ in.), knee-cops, spurs fastened by single straps, sword-belt (2 in.) and sword on left side (13 in. remaining of scabbard). Left arm flattened, and two small holes indicate that shield was attached. Hands in prayer, right leg crossed over left, head on two cushions, and feet on lion (mutilated). Mr. Albert Hartshorne draws attention to this figure being artistically and accurately carved; while the loose fit of the mail about the right arm and neck is well expressed. Effigy in poor state of preservation. See Plate XII, Fig. 27.

REFERENCES. Gough, II, cx; Baker's *Northants*, II, 122; Bridge's *Northants* (1791), I, 282; Hartshorne's *Northants Effigies*, 92 (illustrated); *Victoria Hist. Northants*, I, 402; *Notes and Queries*, 6th S., VIII, 451; *Some Minor Arts*, 64 (illustrated); *Arch. Journ.*, XXV, 251; *Portfolio* (1893), 205 (illustrated); *Archæologia*, LXI, 502, 541.

ASHTON (St. Michael and All Angels). On modern tomb in south-west corner of north aisle.

PERSON REPRESENTED. Sir Philip le Lou, member of ancient family of Lupus. Fought against Scots in 1301, and accounted for fourth part of fee of Ashton and returned as lord of the place in 1315. See Hartshorne's *Northants Effigies*, 91.

EFFIGY (5 ft. 7 in.) in coif of mail, gambeson, hauberk, mail hose, surcoat, cingulum, guige (1½ in.), shield destroyed, sword-belt (2 in.), only fragment of hilt remaining on left side, and knee-cops. Hands in prayer, left leg crossed over right, two low cushions at head, and a lion (decayed) at feet. Figure in sad state of decay. See Plate VI, Fig. 15.

REFERENCES. Gough, II, cx; Bridge's *Northants*, I, 282; Baker's *Northants*, II, 127; Hartshorne's *Northants Effigies*, 99 (illustrated); *Victoria Hist. Northants*, I, 400; *Arch. Journ.*, XXV, 251; *Archæologia*, LXI, 505, 541.

BRAYBROOKE (All Saints'). Placed on tressels in south aisle.

PERSON REPRESENTED. Sir Thomas le Latimer. Summoned to Parliament 1289 and 1310, and died 1334. See Hartshorne's *Northants Effigies*.

EFFIGY (6 ft. 10 in.) in ridged head-piece (seldom met with), camail, hauberk, mail hose, knee-cops of plate, rowel spurs and straps, shield on left arm (2 ft. by 1 ft. 5½ in.), guige, sword-belt (1½ in.), interlaced round scabbard, sword (2 ft. 1½ in.) having hilt with straight quillons, short surcoat open at sides. Hands in plain gauntlets in prayer, right leg crossed over left, moustaches drooping, lion at feet, two cushions under head (damaged). Figure made out of piece of knotty oak. The short surcoat indicates the transitional period from cyclas to jupon, while the ridged head-piece is the precursor of the pointed bascinet. The figure was probably the work of a local carpenter. See Plate XVI, Fig. 35.

REFERENCES. Bridge's *Northants* (1791), II, 13; *Arch. Journ.*, XVIII, 75; XXV, 251; Baker's *Northants*, II, 127; Hartshorne's *Northants Effigies*, 93 (illustrated); *Victoria Hist. Northants*, I, 400; *Some Minor Arts*, 65 (illustrated); *Portfolio* (1893), 206 (illustrated); Prior and Gardner's *Medieval Figure-Sculpture in England*, 667; *Archæologia*, LXI, 500, 506, 541, 542.

COLD HIGHAM (St. Luke). On freestone tomb with delicate tracery panelling under arched recess in south wall of Potcote Chapel.

PERSON REPRESENTED. Sir John Pateshull or Pattishall (? 1291–1349). Summoned to council of magnates, 1335 (*Fœdera*, II, 916), to Parliament 1342, and to military service in 1345 (*Ib.*, III, 52). See *Dict. Nat. Biog.*, XLIV, 30.

EFFIGY (6 ft. 3 in.) in bascinet and camail, hauberk, mail hose, knee-cops, elbow-cops with single articulations, spurs and straps, long surcoat to below knees, left hand on scabbard (1 ft. 5 in. remaining), sword-belt (2 in.) attached to scabbard by lockets, hands in leather gloves, two cushions under head, and lion (mutilated) at feet. This is a good example of transitional armour ; hauberk, surcoat and mail hose belonging to the early part of fourteenth century, while bascinet, camail, gloves, elbow-pieces, and knee-cops indicate the middle of the century. The two low cushions belong to the earlier period. See Plate XVIII, Fig. 40.

REFERENCES. *Arch. Journ.*, XXV, 251 ; Hartshorne's *Northants Effigies* (illustrated) ; *Victoria Hist. Northants*, I, 405 ; *Archæologia*, LXI, 508, 509, 542.

DODFORD (St. Mary the Virgin). In wall recess in north aisle.

PERSON REPRESENTED. ? Hawise Keynes, mother of Sir Robert Keynes, who was living in 1329.

EFFIGY (6 ft. 7 in.) in kirtle, cote-hardie, wimple and veil falling to shoulders. Hands (supplied as separate piece probably) in prayer ; arms broken at shoulders. This is a melancholy wreck of a once beautiful effigy which was probably made in a London workshop and follows the lines of freestone

effigies, such as the "lady" at Ifield, Sussex. See Plate XIII, Fig. 30.

REFERENCES. Baker's *Northants*, I, 361 ; *Arch. Journ.*, XXV, 251 ; Hartshorne's *Northants Effigies*, 93 (illustrated) ; *Victoria Hist. Northants*, I, 40 ; *Some Minor Arts*, 64 (illustrated) ; *Portfolio* (1893), 206 (illustrated) ; Prior and Gardner's *Medieval Figure-Sculpture in England*, 669 ; *Archæologia*, LXI, 511, 542.

GAYTON (St. Mary the Virgin). Under ogee arch in the wall between chancel and north chapel.

PERSON REPRESENTED. Sir Philip Gayton, 1316.

EFFIGY (5 ft. 10 in.) in coif of mail with fillet round temples, hauberk, long surcoat, cingulum ($\frac{3}{4}$ in.), prick spurs and straps, knee-cops, sword (damaged, 1 ft. 10 in.) ; hands in prayer ; right leg crossed over left. Effigy made probably in London, and carefully and judiciously restored by Dr. Butler, Dean of Peterborough. See Plate XI, Fig. 24.

REFERENCES. Baker's *Northants*, II, 281 ; *Arch. Journ.*, XVIII, 75 ; XXV, 251 ; *Notes and Queries*, 1st S., VIII, 19 ; Hartshorne's *Northants Effigies*, 99 (illustrated) ; Prior and Gardner's *Medieval Figure-Sculpture in England*, 666 ; *Archæologia*, LXI, 505, 542.

HOLDENBY (All Saints').

PERSON REPRESENTED. ? Robert Holdenby, who married Joan, dau. of Richard Zouche, and builder of the greater part of the church. See *Arch. Journ.*, LXV, 97.

EFFIGY destroyed.

(In 1786 Gough mentions this

PLATE XXVI.

Fig. 58.

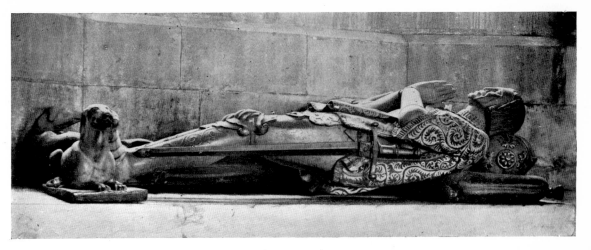

SIR ALEX. CULPEPER (DIED 1537). GOUDHURST, KENT.

Fig. 59.

? ELINOR, WIFE OF THOMAS GAMES (*c.* 1555). BRECON CATHEDRAL.

effigy as " a wooden figure of a man in a buttoned gown." Mr. Justinian Isham (afterwards Sir Justinian Isham, fifth baronet) visited Holdenby 2nd September, 1717, and mentions in his MS. Diary the existence of " an old monument of a person in wood who I was told was a Holdenbie, a helmet and sword lies upon it." There is a local tradition that this effigy, sword and head-piece were taken away many years ago by a gentleman of the neighbourhood, who came in his carriage for the purpose. See *Arch. Jour.*, LXV, 97. It is probable that this effigy belonged to the early part of the reign of Edward III, and represented a franklin *in tunica botonata cum manicis botonatis*. In Bridge's *Northants* (1791) we find that he says the recess in the south wall of the south aisle contained " the wooden statue of a man in a buttoned gown, with an iron sword and head-piece laid by him.")

REFERENCES. Gough, II, cx ; Bridge's *Northants*, I, 529 ; Sir Justinian Isham's private MS. diary, 2nd September, 1717 ; Baker's *Northants*, I, 219, 210 ; *Arch. Journ.*, LXV, 97.

PAULESPURY (St. James). On high freestone tomb under easternmost arch of the chancel aisle on north side.

No. 1. PERSON REPRESENTED. Sir Laurence Pavely, summoned to perform military service beyond the sea in the reign of Edward II ; also summoned to great council at Westminster (17 Ed. II). Obtained confirmation of his lands in 1323, and died 1349.

EFFIGY (6 ft. 1 in.) in conical and fluted bascinet (of excessively rare occurrence), to which a camail is attached by laces running through loops, haketon with tight-fitting sleeves, cyclas with loose sleeves reaching below elbows, mail hose bound with a band below knees, fluted knee-cops, rowel spurs and straps, hands in plain cuffed gauntlets (right holding scabbard and left sheathing sword), left arm bears shield (mutilated 1 ft. 9 in. by 9 in.), sword (1 ft. 6 in. remaining) loosely suspended by belt (2 in.) and fastened by a double locket placed a few inches below top of scabbard, two cushions under head, and feet on lion. Figure shows decline in art ; but has suffered from whitewash and neglect. See Plate XVIII, Fig. 41.

REFERENCES. Gough, VI, cx ; Baker's *Northants*, II, 207 ; *Arch. Jour.*, XXV, 250 ; Hartshorne's *Northants Effigies*, 66 (illustrated) ; *Victoria Hist. Northants*, I, 402 ; *Some Minor Arts*, 65 ; *Portfolio* (1893), 206 (illustrated) ; *Archæologia*, LXI, 506, 507, 513, 543.

No. 2. PERSON REPRESENTED. Dame Pavely (wife of Sir Laurence Pavely), 1350.

EFFIGY (5 ft. 10 in.) in kirtle with tight-fitting sleeves, long sleeveless cotehardie, caught up over arm and falling in graceful folds to feet, wimple, coverchief falling in elegant folds 6 in. below shoulders, and circlet round temples. Hands in prayer, head on two cushions, and dog at feet. This figure is an artistic success and was probably made in London, following the best lines of contemporary freestone effigies. See Plate XVIII, Fig. 42.

REFERENCES. See No. 1 Effigy.

WOODFORD (St. Mary the Virgin). On stone tomb in line of north arcade between chancel and north aisle chapel.

No. 1. PERSON REPRESENTED. ? Sir Walter Treylli, 1290. This family were interested in Woodford from time of Henry II.

EFFIGY (6 ft.) in round head-piece fastened to coif of mail, hauberk, short surcoat reaching just below knees, cingulum, mail hose, knee-cops, guige (1½ in.) and shield (1 ft. 8 in. remaining), sword-belt (1¾ in.), sword (1 ft. 1 in. remaining), suspended by two lockets, and hilt with straight quillons; no spurs (possibly oversight of the sculptor). Hands in prayer, head on two low cushions, and lion at feet. Conjectured that the widow erected this effigy and her own in early years of fourteenth century. Dame Eleanor died 1316. See Plate XI, Fig. 25.

REFERENCES. Gough, II, cvi (illustrated Plate IV); *Antiquaries Museum*, I, 269 (illustrated); Bridge's *Northants Arch. Jour.*, XXV, 250; *Notes and Queries*, 1st S., VIII, 19; Hartshorne's *Northants Effigies*, 91 (illustrated); *Victoria Hist. North-*

ants, I, 401; *Some Minor Arts*, 58 (illustrated); *Portfolio* (1893), 181 (illustrated); Prior and Gardner's *Medieval Figure-Sculpture in England*, 669; *Archæologia*, LXI, 493, 502, 511, 543.

No. 2. PERSON REPRESENTED. ? Dame Eleanor Treylli (wife of above), died 1316.

EFFIGY (5 ft. 10 in.) in kirtle with tight-fitting sleeves, sleeveless cote-hardie gathered up under left arm, mantle, deep wimple, coverchief falling in most graceful folds, pointed shoes, hands in prayer, two low cushions under head, and dog at feet. The mantle has been diapered in two shades of red and white in alternate quatrefoils containing concentric foliations and circles intermittently, decorated with swans and cinquefoils, with the same floral centres of a smaller size. See *Victoria Hist. Northants*, I, 401. Draperies and folds of kirtle, mantle and coverchief are not only skilfully arranged but artistically carved. Effigy probably made in a London atelier and based on such a figure as the stone effigy of a "lady" at Ifield, Sussex, or an example of one at Leckhampton, Gloucestershire. See Plate XI, Fig. 25.

REFERENCES. See No. 1 Effigy.

NOTTINGHAMSHIRE

LAXTON (St. Michael). Placed on founder's tomb with her husband and his first wife, on north side of chancel.

PERSON REPRESENTED. Margaret, second wife of Adam of Everingham. She

survived her husband, who died in 1287.

EFFIGY (5 ft. 8 in.) in wimple, veil falling to shoulders, confined round head by circlet, long loose kirtle and mantle caught up under arm. Hands in prayer. Date *c.* 1290. Good work and carved most likely in a London atelier. See Plate II, Fig. 4.

REFERENCES. *Arch. Journ.*, XVIII, 75; Letter C. E. S. Foljambe; *Thornton Soc. Trans.*, IV, 1902 (illustrated); Prior and Gardner's *Medieval Figure-Sculpture in England*, 668; *Archæologia*, LXI, 500, 501, 511, 544.

NOTTINGHAM.

PERSON REPRESENTED. A hermit or anchorite.

EFFIGY destroyed.

(A decayed wooden effigy was found in 1818 when cleaning out an old hermitage in the west face of Standard Hill rock, Nottingham. A grave was found containing human remains as well as the effigy. See *The Gentleman's Magazine*, 10th May, 1818; *The Nottingham Guardian*, 15th April, 1905.)

RADCLIFFE-ON-TRENT (Parish Church).

PERSON REPRESENTED. Stephen Radcliffe, Lord of the Manor.

EFFIGY destroyed.

(The story of the loss of this effigy is given by William Stretton, of Nottingham, who flourished in the early part of last century and who visited Radcliffe Church in 1824. He writes: " The church has undergone considerable alteration, about the year 1793." " An arched recess under the south wall has formerly been occupied by a figure which was destroyed in the alterations of 1793." " Stephen Radcliffe, a prostrate figure carved in wood, used to lye under an arch in the south front of the church, he was lord of the manor, and patron of the living; he is supposed to have lain there for many generations, until the rejoicings took place on the death of Tom Paine, when a number of youths stole him away and burnt him as an effigy in lieu of Payne." This extract is published in *The Churches of Notts* (Bingham Hundred), 394–95; *History of Lenton*, 463.)

RUTLAND

ASHWELL (St. Mary the Virgin). On floor of south chapel.

PERSON REPRESENTED. ? Knight of the Touchet family, possibly Robert or Thomas Touchet. This family held the Manor of Ashwell from reign of Edward II.

EFFIGY (6 ft. 1 in.) in hauberk with gambeson beneath, mail hose, surcoat reaching to knees, cingulum, coif of mail with narrow fillet round temples, sword-belt (2 in.) with sword (1 ft. 11 in. remaining) on left side, spurs

(pricks gone) and straps. Hands in prayer, right leg crossed over left, lion (mutilated) at feet, and two cushions under head. Face, hands, and other portions somewhat decayed.

REFERENCES. *Arch. Journ.*, XVIII, 75; *Notes and Queries*, 1st S., VII, 607; Wright's *Rutland* (Touchet family); *Archæologia*, LXI, 505, 544.

TICKENCOTE (St. Peter). In recess in south wall of chancel.

PERSON REPRESENTED. ? Sir Roland le

G

Dameys, knighted 1355. In king's service in French wars. Represented his county in Great Council at Westminster 1352, and thrice in Parliament. Living in 1388.

EFFIGY (6 ft. 5 in.) in bascinet with camail, hauberk, jupon with fringe of fleurs-de-lys, shoulder-pieces, brassarts, vambraces, elbow-cops, thigh-pieces, jambs, knee-cops, articulated sollerets, richly ornamented baldrick (2 in.); no spurs or sword. Hands in prayer, dog at feet, and cushion under head. Figure in poor and defaced condition. The figure was removed from the tomb of Sir Roland le Dameys when the chapel of the Holy Trinity was demolished at the Reformation.

REFERENCES. Wright's *Rutland* (Dameys family); Blore's *Rutland*, 74; *Notes and Queries*, 1st S., VII, 528; Barton's *Guide to Tickencote*; *Archæologia*, LXI, 508, 545.

SHROPSHIRE

BERRINGTON (All Saints'). In south wall recess under segmental arch in south aisle.

PERSON REPRESENTED. ? Knight of the Berrington family.

EFFIGY (6 ft. 2 in.) in mail coif with narrow fillet round temple, hauberk showing quilted gambeson beneath, mail hose, knee-cops, surcoat reaching below knees, cingulum, sword-belt (2 in.) attached to scabbard, on left (1 ft. 1 in. of sword remaining), spurs (pricks gone) and straps, hands in prayer, right leg crossed over left, head on two cushions, and feet on lion. Figure dates from early years of fourteenth century, probably made in a London workshop. Face damaged and sword broken. See Plate X, Fig. 22.

REFERENCES. Eyton's *Shropshire*, VI, 282; Anderson's *Shropshire*, 204; Cranage's *Churches of Shropshire*, 467; *Archæologia*, LXI, 494, 495, 501, 545; Anden's *Shropshire*, 68.

BURFORD (St. Mary the Virgin). On wooden table-tomb in middle of chancel.

PERSON REPRESENTED. Edmund Cornewall, son and heir of Sir Thomas Cornewall. Died in his twentieth year (1508).

EFFIGY (6 ft. 1 in.) in plate armour: cuirass, taces (4), tuilles with mail skirt beneath, shoulder-pieces, brassarts, elbow-cops, vambraces, gorget of plate, thigh-pieces, knee-cops, with articulated plates above and below, jambs, articulated sabbatons, hands (uncovered) in prayer, no sword nor spurs, head uncovered, long hair falling to neck, face clean-shaven, two angels on helmet support head with their hands, crowned dog at feet. Tomb and figure repainted in recent years. Compare armour with Sir Henry Vernon (Tong), but tuilles not so large and elaborate. See Plate XXIII, Figs. 52 and 53.

REFERENCES. *Notes and Queries*, IX, 62; Timmins's *Nooks and Corners of Shropshire*, 209; Cranage's *Churches of Shropshire*, 241–3 (illustrated), Plate XXXI; *Archæologia*, LXI, 513, 545.

PLATE XXVII.

Fig. 60.

ANTHONY ST. LEGER (*c.* 1540). SLYNDON, SUSSEX.

Fig. 61.

DETAILS OF CHILDREN ON WOODEN TOMB-CHEST, HENRY NEVILLE, FIFTH
EARL OF WESTMORLAND (1564). STAINDROP, CO. DURHAM.

Fig. 62.

WILLIAM (DIED 1587) AND ALICE (DIED 1579) POLEY. BOXTED, SUFFOLK.

EATON-UNDER-HEYWOOD (St. Edith). In recess in south wall of chancel with beautiful cinquefoiled canopy and attached shafts with capitals of natural foliage. Its decorated character is shown by the mouldings, especially the scroll and the ball-flower ornament.

PERSON REPRESENTED. ? Lord of Manor, *c.* 1350.

(The ball-flower ornament on tomb is not inconsistent with such a date.)

EFFIGY (6 ft. 2 in.) in close-fitting hood, long cote concealing under-tunic, shoes with pointed toes, hands in prayer. Good work, but probable that hands and head have been restored to some extent. One cushion under head ; no support for feet. See Plate XX, Fig. 46.

REFERENCES. Cranage's *Churches of Shropshire*, 194 ; *Archæologia*, LXI, 497, 545.

HIGH ERCALL.

PERSON REPRESENTED. ? Some knight of the Ercall family. Sir William Ercall is called *clericus.* Died 1304 ; John Ercall living in 1311.

EFFIGY destroyed.

In mail coif, hauberk, showing gambeson beneath, mail hose, long surcoat, cingulum, guige with kite-shaped shield on left arm, right leg crossed over left, broad sword-belt, right hand holds sword (broken), head on two cushions and lion at feet.

REFERENCES. The late Rev. C. H. Hartshorne made a sketch of this effigy in 1835, showing that it existed at that date.

PITCHFORD (St. Michael). On wooden chest on south side of chancel.

PERSON REPRESENTED. Sir John Pitchford (1237–1285), son of Ralf de Pitchford. Patent dated 11th July, 1266, spared him the consequences of rebellion. In 1273 he appeared before King's Council, giving evidence as to age of George Cantilupe, then claiming his livery. Married Margaret Devereux.

EFFIGY (7 ft. 1 in.) in mail coif with fillet round temples, hauberk, surcoat reaching below knees, mail hose, cingulum, guige, but no shield now, right leg crossed over left, spurs (pricks gone) and straps, sword-belt (2 in.) with pendant of 1 ft. 10 in. beyond buckle, sword 1 in. out of scabbard (4 ft.), right hand on pommel of sword, one cushion under head, and a lion at feet with tail between legs curled over back, holding end of scabbard in mouth. Effigy made probably in a London workshop. Excellent figure in good preservation. The tomb on which the effigy lies is adorned with trefoil-headed arches (7) containing heater-shaped shields emblazoned with armorial bearings. For description, see Eyton's *Shropshire*, VI, 282. The heraldry clearly indicates that the effigy represents Sir John de Pitchford. North panel much later, displays Tudor rose and small Tudor flowers, probably part of a late Perpendicular screen. See Plate II, Fig. 3.

REFERENCES. *Arch. Journ.*, XVIII, 75 ; Eyton's *Shropshire*, VI, 282 (illustrated) ; Anderson's *Shropshire* (illustrated) ; Timmins's *Nooks and Corners of Shropshire*, 41 (illustrated) ; Cranage's *Churches of Shropshire*,

503 ; *Portfolio* (1893), 207 ; Prior and Gardner's *Medieval Figure-Sculpture in England*, 664 ; Crossley's *English Church Monuments*, 181 (illustrated), 209 ; *Archæologia*, LXI, 500, 546.

SOMERSET

CHEW MAGNA (St. Andrew). In recess in south wall of nave.

PERSON REPRESENTED. ? John Wych, died 1346. Tradition ascribes this effigy to Sir John Hauteville ; but he lived in the reign of Henry III, and this figure was carved between 1340 to 1350. The last Hauteville was Geoffrey, who parted with the Manor of Norton to John Wych in 1328.

EFFIGY (5 ft. 9 in.) in transitional armour (1340 to 1350), helmet, hauberk, shoulder-pieces, brassarts, elbow-cops, vambraces, thigh-pieces, knee-cops, jambs, sollerets, prick spurs and straps, surcoat, cingulum, guige, sword-belt (1¾ to 2 in.) and gauntlets with gadlings. Knight reclines on left side resting on hip and left elbow, and between left elbow and hip lies shield (2 ft. 3 in. by 1 ft. 2 in.), right arm brought over breast, and hand rests on edge of shield, left leg raised from hip, and foot placed on roaring lion. The feet show the toes and are probably encased in thin leathers fitting like gloves. Figure repainted and restored in recent years by the Rev. Rawdon W. Hauteville. Figure brought from Norton Hauteville Chapel when that church was demolished at the Reformation. Effigy made, probably, at Abingdon in Berkshire. See Plate XVI, Fig. 36.

REFERENCES. Gough, II, cxi ; Collinson's *Somerset*, II, 108 ; *Notes and Queries*, 1st S., VIII, 604 ; *Arch. Jour.*, XIV, 158 (illustrated), 226 (illustrated) ; Paul's *Sepulchral Effigies in N.W. Somerset*, 7 ; *Proc. Som. Arch. Soc.*, 21–25, 31, 32, Pl. IV ; *Archæologia*, LXI, 493, 494, 509, 546 ; Prior and Gardner's *Medieval Figure-Sculpture in England*, 352, 554, 670.

MIDSOMER NORTON (St. John Baptist). In the Belfry.

PERSON REPRESENTED. ? Knight of the Warknell family.

EFFIGY (present length 4 ft. 11 in.) in coif of mail, hauberk, surcoat, cingulum, shield (1 ft. 11 in. by 1 ft. 2 in.) on left arm. Legs destroyed and figure sadly mutilated. Gough (1796) says effigy was in south aisle, but originally rested on raised tomb under singers' gallery. This refers to the old church ; new church built 1830. Effigy made, probably, in Bristol.

REFERENCES. Gough, II, cx ; Collinson's *Somerset*, II, 151 ; *Proc. Som. Arch. Soc.*, LXII, 57–59, 79. Sketch in Braikenridge's illustrated *Collinson*, II, Part I, 151 ; sketch in Adlam's illustrated *Collinson* (*Soc. Ant.*), IV, 151 ; *Archæologia*, LXI, 494, 547.

PLATE XXVIII.

Fig. 63.

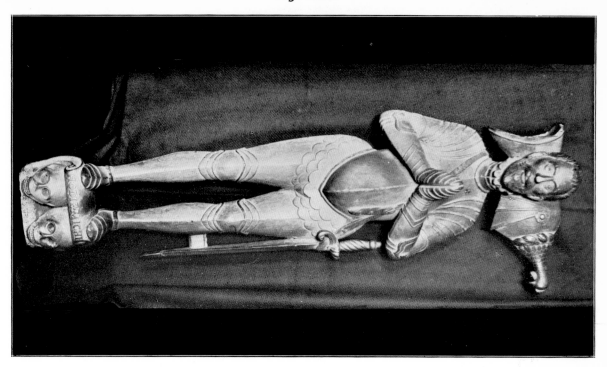

JOHN HEATH OF KEPIER (DIED 1590).   ST. GILES', DURHAM.

Fig. 64.

? LADY ELIZABETH PHILPOTTS.   THRUXTON, HAMPSHIRE.

STAFFORDSHIRE

WESTON-UNDER-LYZARD (St. Andrew). In recess in south wall of chancel.

No. 1. PERSON REPRESENTED. ? Sir Hugh Weston, 1305.

EFFIGY (5 ft. 10 in.) in mail coif with fillet round temples, hauberk showing quilted gambeson beneath, mail hose, knee-cops, long surcoat, cingulum (1 in.), rowel spurs, sword-belt (2½ in.) passed round scabbard of sword (3 ft. 11 in.) possessing hilt with straight quillons. Hands in prayer (bare) ; one holds hilt and one placed on scabbard ; right leg crossed over left, two cushions under head, and lion at feet. Good work.

REFERENCES. *Arch. Journ.*, XVIII, 320 ; *Notes and Queries*, 6th S., VII, 451 ; VIII, 398 ; *William Salt Arch. Soc.*, N.S., II, " Hist. Coll. Staffordshire " ; C. H. Hartshorne's *Domestic Manners during Reign of Edward I*, 35 ; *Portfolio* (1893), 207 ; *Archæologia*, LXI, 503, 504, 547.

No. 2. PERSON REPRESENTED. ? Sir John Weston. In 1297 accompanied Elizabeth, Countess of Holland and Hereford, as her attorney, when she went to Flanders with her father, Edward I. Sir John had charge of her jewels, and it has been conjectured that the little purse slung from his cingulum denotes his badge of office. Such a purse on a military effigy is very rare. However, there is one of somewhat this size on stone effigies of knights at High Ercall and Leighton-under-Lyzard. The effigy at Weston-under-Lyzard and Leighton-under-Wrekin are within a 15-mile radius of High Ercall. Sir John de Weston died soon after his return from Flanders.

EFFIGY (5 ft. 8 in.) in mail coif, hauberk and hose, knee-cops, surcoat reaching below knees, girdle, to which is hung a small purse (5 in. by 4 in.), guige, but no shield, rowel spurs and straps, right hand sheathing sword, left holding scabbard, right leg crossed over left, head on one cushion, lion at feet holding right leg of knight. Good work and much care bestowed on details ; both figures in good preservation. Effigy in recess in north wall of chancel.

REFERENCES. See No. 1 Effigy.

SUFFOLK

BOXTED (All Saints'). On brick tomb protected by railings in recess in south wall.

No. 1. PERSON REPRESENTED. William Poley, 1587.

EFFIGY (6 ft.) in complete plate armour, no spurs, tassets over trunk hose, ornamented belt with sword (3 ft. 5 in.) attached to left side, ruffs round neck and wrists, hands in prayer, head uncovered, hair curly, beard long and divided into two points, moustaches long and drooping. No support for feet. Head on tilting helmet. Well preserved, painted black. See Plate XXVII, Fig. 62.

REFERENCES. *Notes and Queries*, 1st S., IX, 457 ; Davey's MS. Coll. (B.M.),

19077, f. 124; *Proc. Suffolk Inst. of Arch.*, III, Note to Plate I and p. 366; *Archæologia*, LXI, 518, 548.

No. 2. PERSON REPRESENTED. Alice Poley, wife of above, dau. and heiress of Edmund Shaa, of Horndon House, Essex. Died 1579.

EFFIGY (5 ft. 6 in.) in gown high at neck, gathered in pleats at waist, divided in front, showing petticoat with two bands of trimming at bottom, loose sleeves gathered at shoulders, ruffs round neck and wrists, prayer book (5 in. by 2½ in. by 1 in.) hung from girdle adorned with lozenge of Poley arms (*or—a lion rampant sable*) impaling Shaa (*azure a chevron between three lozenges ermine*), hands in prayer, head in jewelled French cap, three chains round neck, narrow chain bracelets, at feet a greyhound, head on ornamental cushion (top *dexter* BEATI MORTUI QUI IN DOMINO MORIUNTUR, *sinister* a device and A.D. 1579, March 7). Figure well preserved, painted black. See Plate XXVII, Fig. 62.

REFERENCES. See No. 1 Effigy.

BURES (St. Mary the Virgin). Under second window of north aisle.

PERSON REPRESENTED. ? A knight, said to be a Corne, or Cornard. Tradition ascribes his sale of Corn Hall in drunken freak and his burial in wall of church to the reign of Henry III; but figure is about 1330 and in relationship with some alabaster effigies of that date, and carved, probably, in London.

EFFIGY (5 ft. 7 in.) in mail coif, hauberk showing gambeson beneath, mail hose, knee-cops, surcoat, cingulum, guige (1¾ in.), shield (1 ft. 7 in. by 1 ft. 3¾ in.) on left arm, sword-belt (1¾ in.) and sword (fragment 1 ft. 9¾ in.), possessing hilt with straight quillons on left side, right leg crossed over left, rowel spurs and straps, hands in prayer, lion at feet, head on cushions supported by two angels, both vested in albs, and one in cope. Head of angels and portions of figure have suffered from time and neglect. See Plate XIV, Fig. 31.

REFERENCES. Gough, I, cxviii; Davy's MS. Coll. (B.M.), 19077, f. 170; Jervis's *Coronation of St. Edmund*, 5; *Brit. Arch. Assoc. Jour.*, XXXII, 416; Prior and Gardner's *Medieval Figure-Sculpture in England*, 667, Fig. 748; *Archæologia*, LXI, 494, 504, 548.

HEVENINGHAM (St. Margaret). Originally on high tomb with effigy of lady against north wall of north chapel. After destruction of chapel placed in belfry, now on floor of church.

No. 1. PERSON REPRESENTED. ? Knight of the Heveningham family. Some authorities conjecture it was Sir John Heveningham, died 1452 or 1453. This figure is in a jupon, so it could not represent Sir John, as the fashion went out about 1410.

EFFIGY (6 ft.) in cuirass covered by jupon, hauberk shoulder-pieces, brassarts, elbow-pieces, vambraces, taces, thigh-pieces, knee-cops, jambs, sollerets, spurs (gone) and straps, baudrick (2½ in.), sword (destroyed), head in helmet with visor raised, drooping moustaches, arms broken, but hands were in prayer, support for head and feet lost, and figure mutilated, having suffered from neglect and decay.

REFERENCES. Gough, I, cxix ; Davy's MS. Coll. (B.M.), 19081, f. 64, 65 ; Weever ; Suckling's *Suffolk*, II, 395 (illustrated) ; *Brit. Arch. Assoc. Jour.*, XXXII, 416 ; *Archæologia*, XLVI, 280 ; LXI, 508, 549.

No. 2. PERSON REPRESENTED. ? Elizabeth, dau. and heiress of Sir John Ridisham, and wife of Sir John Heveningham. Suckling's *Suffolk*, II, 395, says that original tomb had shield of arms of Heveningham and Ridisham.

EFFIGY destroyed.

(Gough mentions effigy in 1786 (I, xcix) ; Davy (MS. Coll. (B.M.), 19081, f. 64, 65) speaks of it as sadly mutilated in 1833. A few years later it had disappeared.)

REFERENCES. See No. 1 Effigy.

No. 3. PERSON REPRESENTED. ? A lady of the Heveningham family.

EFFIGY destroyed.

(Weever who wrote in 1631 speaks of this effigy as " curiously painted and gilt.")

REFERENCES. Weever ; Suckling's *Suffolk*, II, 395.

WINGFIELD (St. Andrew). High tomb under easternmost arch between south chapel and chancel.

No. 1. PERSON REPRESENTED. Michael de la Pole, 2nd Earl of Suffolk (? 1361–1415), knighted 1377, obtained annulment of his father's outlawry, attended Council of Westminster several times, commissioner for trial of Earl of Cambridge, Lord le Scrope, and Sir Thomas Gray, and died of dysentery during siege of Harfleur. See *Gesta Henrici Quinti*, 31 (Eng. Hist. Soc.) ; Nicholas's *Testamenta Vetusta*, 189 ; *Dict. Nat. Biog.*, XLVI, 33.

EFFIGY (6 ft. 6 in.) in armour of transitional period. Cuirass covered by jupon, hauberk, gorget of plate, bascinet, camail, articulated shoulder-pieces, brassarts, elbow-cops, vambraces, taces, knee-cops, jambs, sollerets, hands in prayer, in cuffed gauntlets with gadlings, broad belt, but no sword or sword-belt, moustaches long and drooping, head on tilting helmet with crest, and lion at feet. Figure carved, probably, in London with great care. The north side of the tomb on which this and the following effigy lie forms the sedilia for high altar ; south side once contained figures of Earl's children, and names were painted on ledge above. The Stafford knot (badge of the Countess's family) freely used in adornment of tomb and arch above. See plate XXI, Fig. 48.

REFERENCES. Gough, I, xcix ; Davy's MS. Coll., 19092, f. 199 ; *Proc. Suffolk Inst. of Arch.*, III, 335 ; *Some Minor Arts*, 66 (illustrated) ; Stothard's *Monumental Effigies*, 84 (illustrated in three plates) ; *Portfolio* (1893), 206 (illustrated) ; Prior and Gardner's *Medieval Figure-Sculpture in England*, 670, Fig. 753 ; Crossley's *English Church Monuments* (illustrated), 22 ; *Archæologia*, LXI, 509, 510, 549.

No. 2. PERSON REPRESENTED. Catherine Stafford, dau. of Hugh, Earl of Stafford, and wife of above.

EFFIGY (5 ft. 10 in.) in kirtle, cotehardie, long mantle with deep collar and folds caught up over arms, broad belt and buckle, head-dress having fret of fine pattern of four-leaved flowers set in squares, and circlet enclosing veil falling to neck, pointed shoes, hands in prayer, head on two cushions and lioness at feet. Excellent figure well preserved. Both figures shrouded in paint about one hundred years ago. This beautiful effigy was made most likely in a London atelier and may be compared with the effigy of Margaret Holland between her two husbands in Canterbury Cathedral. See Plate XX, Fig. 47.

SURREY

SOUTHWARK (St. Saviour's Cathedral Church). In a wall recess of north aisle of quire.

PERSON REPRESENTED. ? Knight of the Warenne family. This family were benefactors to the Priory of St. Mary, Overy (*Monasticon*, VI, 172).

EFFIGY (6 ft. 6½ in.) in mail coif, hauberk with long sleeves covering hands in mittens, showing gambeson beneath, mail hose, spurs (pricks gone) and straps, long surcoat, cingulum, guige, but no shield, swordbelt (1½ in.), right hand holds scabbard, left placed on pommel of sword and sheathing blade, left leg crossed over right, cushion under head and lion at feet. Figure, ? 1290–1300, has been restored (? by Richardson), face modern. Originally this was, doubtless, an excellent figure; it is now difficult to know extent of restoration. It was, however, made in London and is a copy of the latest Purbeck marble treatment. See Plate V, Fig. 11.

REFERENCES. Gough, I, xcix; Manning and Bray, 373 (illustrated); Grose, *Ant.*, pref., Plate III, Fig. 2; Thompson's *Hist. of St. Saviour's*, 110, 113 (illustrated); Brayley and Britton's *Hist. of Surrey*, V, 364; Prior and Gardner's *Medieval Figure-Sculpture in England*, 664, Fig. 743; *Archæologia*, LXI, 495, 550.

SUSSEX

SLYNDON (St. Mary the Virgin). On modern high tomb at east end of south aisle, formerly in Tudor recess, south side of chancel.

PERSON REPRESENTED. ? Sir Anthony Kempe a grantee of the Manor in 1553, or to Anthony St. Ledger (locally "Sellinger"), whose will, dated 1539, directs his burial to be in Slyndon Church. The style of the armour indicates that the latter appropriation is, probably, the correct one.

EFFIGY (5 ft. 2 in.) in plate armour,

PLATE XXIX.

Fig. 65.

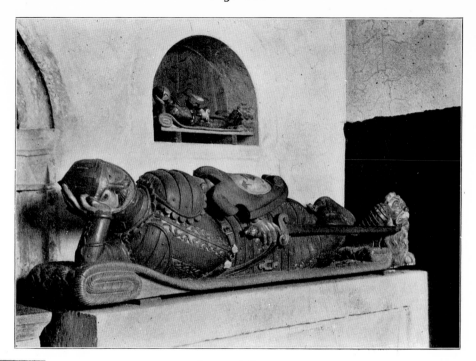

SIR WILLIAM OGLANDER (DIED 1608). BRADING, ISLE OF WIGHT.

Fig. 66.

SIR JOHN OGLANDER (DIED 1655) AND GEORGE OGLANDER, SON. BRADING, ISLE OF WIGHT.

uncovered hands in prayer, no sword or spurs, hair long, in clubbed form, head on tilting helmet, and no support for feet. The armour is a good example of the middle Tudor period ; the vambraces are fluted and tuilles channelled. The protuberant guard of the fork of the legs and the peculiar shaped broad-toed sabbatons (Renaissance in the scrolling) denote contemporary fashions. The elbow and knee-cops also show Renaissance work. See Plate XXVII, Fig. 60.

REFERENCES. Gough, II, cx ; Dallaway's *Western Sussex*, I, 151 ; *Notes and Queries*, 6th S., VIII, 118 ; Horsfield's *Sussex*, II, 68 ; *Archæologia*, LXI, 515, 550 ; *Country Life*, L, 886 (illustrated).

WILTSHIRE

STEEPLE LANGFORD (All Saints').

PERSON REPRESENTED. The Rev. Joseph Collier, M.A., Rector of Steeple Langford from 1607 to 1635.

EFFIGY (2 ft. 11 in.) painted half-figure erect in cassock with girdle, collar, cuffs and skull-cap, beard and moustaches, hands clasping a small red-bound book. The effigy is now placed in a niche over the vestry door, but when Hoare wrote his *History of Wiltshire* in 1825 it was on the south wall of the sanctuary in an elaborate wooden frame surmounted by a skull with a reclining skeleton as a *Memento mori* above the inscription.

REFERENCES. Hoare's *Wiltshire* (1825), II, 13 (illustrated), Plate II ; *Wiltshire Archæological Magazine*, XXXV, 386.

YORKSHIRE

ALLERTON MAULEVERER (St. Martin). On modern deal support in north chapel.

No. 1. PERSON REPRESENTED ? Knight of Mauleverer family.

EFFIGY (6 ft. 4 in.) in head-piece strapped to mail coif, hauberk, mailhose, spurs (pricks gone) and straps, surcoat, cingulum, knee-cops, sword belt (2¼ in.) with sword (fragment 2 ft.) attached on left side, right leg crossed over left, hands in prayer, two cushions under head and lion at feet. Figure sadly worm-eaten and decayed.

REFERENCES. Hargrave's *Knaresborough* (1832), 281 ; Whitaker's *Loidis et Elmete*, 322 (illustrated) ; *Archæologia*, LXI, 505, 551.

No. 2. PERSON REPRESENTED. ? Knight of Mauleverer family.

EFFIGY (present length 5 ft. 2 in.) in mail coif, hauberk, and mail hose, knee-cops, surcoat, cingulum (1 in.), sword, belt (fragment), right leg crossed over left, kite-shaped shield on left arm with fingers holding strap, cushion under head, and support for feet destroyed. Figure sadly worm-eaten and decayed.

REFERENCES. See No. 1 Effigy.

BARNBOROUGH (St. Peter). On tomb of Sir Percival Cresacre (living 1455) and Dame Alice, his wife.

PERSON REPRESENTED. ? Sir Thomas Cresacre, living 1344.

EFFIGY (7 ft. 2½ in.) in basinet, camail, hauberk, gambeson, cyclas, articulated shoulder-pieces, brassarts, elbow-cops, vambraces, thigh-pieces, knee-cops, jambs, articulated sollerets, rowel spurs and straps, hands in gauntlets holding heart between open palms, shield (2 ft. by 1 ft. 2 in.) on left arm, sword (1 ft. 9 in. damaged) possessing hilt with straight quillons and large pommel (2½ in. diameter) attached to ornamented baldrick on left side, head on two cushions and lion at feet. This is one of the finest examples of a wooden effigy, and is well preserved. The fashion of wearing a cyclas lasted from about 1321 to 1346, so that this is one of the latest examples. This effigy in detail and posture resembles the Caen stone "knight" at Ifield (Sussex) and was made, probably, in London. See Plate XVII, Figs. 38 and 39.

REFERENCES. Miller's *Doncaster*, 274; Hunter's *South Yorkshire*, I, 373; Allen's *Yorkshire*, V, 266; Prior and Gardner's *Medieval Figure-Sculpture in England*, 607, Fig. 751; *Archæologia*, LXI, 449, 507, 551.

THORNHILL (St. Michael). At west end of north chapel.

No. 1. PERSON REPRESENTED. Sir John Saville, 1529.

EFFIGY (6 ft. 2 in.) in plate armour, hands in cuffed gauntlets in prayer. Head in helmet, raised visor with rosettes covering hinges, hair long, falling to neck, cushion under head and at feet. Sir John lies between his two wives on wooden tomb adorned with shields of arms in square panels with inscription on edge, "Bonys emong stonys lys here ful styl qwylste the sawle wanderis were that God wyl in Anno DM mill(es)imo quingentissimo vigesimo nono." Figure considerably restored. See Plate XXV, Fig. 56.

REFERENCES. Allen's *Yorkshire*, III, 302; Whitaker's *Loidis et Elmete*, 322 (illustrated); *Notes and Queries*, 6th S., VII, 451; *Portfolio* (1893), 207; *Archæologia*, LXI, 514, 551.

No. 2. PERSON REPRESENTED. Alice Saville (born Vernon), first wife of above.

EFFIGY (5 ft. 10 in.) in kirtle, tight-fitting sleeves with bands at wrists, ornamental border at neck, long mantle fastened with ornamental band and two fastenings, wavy hair falling to elbows, long veil with fillet round temples adorned with deeply-carved Tudor roses, hands in prayer, low cushion under head and no support for feet. Figure on right side of husband.

REFERENCES. See No. 1 Effigy.

No. 3. PERSON REPRESENTED. Dame

Elizabeth Saville (born Paston), second wife of above.

EFFIGY (6 ft.) similar to above lady and placed on left side of husband. See Plate XXV, Fig. 56.

REFERENCES. See No. 1 Effigy.

WHORLTON (Holy Cross). On tomb of later date on north side of chancel, beneath arch into north chapel (now destroyed).

PERSON REPRESENTED. Unknown knight.

EFFIGY (6 ft.) in mail coif with narrow fillet round temples, hauberk, mail hose, knee-cops of plate or leather, long surcoat reaching nearly to ankles, cingulum (1 in.) having long pendant strap below buckle of 2 ft. 10 in. looped over sword-belt, sword in scabbard (1 ft. 3 in. remaining) hangs nearly in front of knight, right leg crossed over left, hands (uncovered) in prayer, feet appear as if uncovered showing the toes, yet they have been armed with spurs (pricks gone) and straps. It has been suggested by Sir William Hope that the feet were encased in their leathers, like gloves, as spurs could hardly have been worn on bare ankles. Head on two cushions, dog at feet. Figure in good preservation; excellent work, carved in London probably between the years 1305 to 1310. See Plate VII, Fig. 16.

REFERENCES. Prior and Gardner's *Medieval Figure-Sculpture in England; Archæologia*, LXI, 504, 552.

WORSBOROUGH (St. Mary the Virgin). Between chancel and south chapel under south arcade.

No. 1. PERSON REPRESENTED. Sir Roger Rockley, son of Sir Thomas Rockley, twice married, and died 1522. Inscription on monument lost, but Dodsworth in 1619 records fragment, "Hic jacet Rogerus Rockley, miles . . . filius Thomae Rockley, militis."

EFFIGY (5 ft. 2 in.) in plate armour, helmet with visor raised, gorget of plate, hands in prayer, hair worn long, face clean-shaven, sword (3 ft. 1 in.) suspended from narrow belt (1 in.) on left side, head on two cushions, and upright semicircular cushion at feet. Crudely repainted in 1836 by local man in Barnsley. On a wooden monument or hearse, consisting of chest with two tiers above it. Chest adorned with five shields. (Rockley twice, Rockley impaling Mountency once, and two uncharged shields.) Cadaver on chest, effigy on first tier, while top tier forms the canopy projecting 2 in. and adorned with trefoils in circles united with a running scroll. See Plate XXIV, Figs. 54 and 55.

REFERENCES. Dodsworth (16th October, 1619); Hunter's *South Yorkshire*, II, 295; Wilkinson's *Worsborough* (illustrated); *Archæologia*, LXI, 493, 514, 552.

No. 2. PERSON REPRESENTED. See No. 1 Effigy.

EFFIGY. Male cadaver laid on shroud, low cushion under head and upright semicircular cushion at feet. Length 5 ft. 2 in.

REFERENCES. See No. 1 Effigy.

INDEX

Printed in Great Britain for ELLIOT STOCK, *Publisher,* 7, PATERNOSTER ROW, LONDON, E.C., *by* BUTLER & TANNER LTD., FROME.